WRITERS AND THEIR WORK

ISOBEL ARMSTRONG
General Editor

DOUGLAS DUNN

DOUGLAS DUNN

David Kennedy

© Copyright 2008 by David Kennedy
First published in 2008 by Northcote House Publishers Ltd,
Horndon, Tavistock, Devon, PL19 9NQ, United Kingdom.
Tel: +44 (0) 1822 810066 Fax: +44 (0) 1822 810034.

All rights reserved. No part of this work may be reproduced or stored in an information retrieval system (other than short extracts for the purposes of review) without the express permission of the Publishers given in writing.

British Library Cataloguing-in-Publication Data
A catalogue record for this book is available from the British Library

ISBN 978-0-7463-1159-2 hardcover
ISBN 978-0-7463-1164-6 paperback
Typeset by PDQ Typesetting, Newcastle-under-Lyme
Printed and bound in the United Kingdom

For Christine

Contents

Acknowledgements	viii
Biographical Outline	ix
Abbreviations and References	xiv
Introduction	1
1 Part of a Place	9
2 Realisms, Rhapsodies and Responsibilities	22
3 Gestures of Affront	37
4 Innermost Dialects	55
5 Decencies, Disenchantments and Diversity	70
Notes	81
Bibliography	86
Index	90

Acknowledgements

I wish to thank Isobel Armstrong for commissioning this book and Douglas Dunn for his support and graciousness in answering my many questions. I am deeply indebted to my wife Christine who has encouraged and sustained me throughout the writing process. Finally, my publishers and I are grateful to Douglas Dunn and Faber and Faber Ltd for permission to quote from the works of Douglas Dunn.

Biographical Outline

1942	Douglas Eaglesham Dunn, born in Inchinnan, Renfrewshire, Scotland, 23 October.
1945	At a by-election in Motherwell, Dr. Robert D. McIntyre becomes the first ever Scottish Nationalist MP.
1946–59	Educated at Inchinnan Primary School; Renfrew High School; and Camphill Senior Secondary School.
1959–62	Library Assistant, Renfrew County Libraries.
1961	Scottish School of Librarianship.
1962–4	Library Assistant, Andersonian Library, Royal College of Science and Technology (now Strathclyde University), Glasgow.
1963	First published poem, 'Apostate on the Rock', appears in *Outposts*.
1964	Labour, under new leader Harold Wilson, win the October General Election.
1964	Marries Lesley Balfour Wallace in November.
1964–6	Dunn and Lesley fly to the USA where he takes up a job as Assistant Librarian, Akron Public Library, Ohio, USA.
1965	Called up for US armed forces due to being on an immigrant's visa as required by Akron Public Library regulations.
1966	Labour, under Harold Wilson, win the March General Election.
1966	Dunn and Lesley return to Scotland. Librarian of Joseph Black Chemistry Library, University of Glasgow.
1966–9	Attends University of Hull. Moves to Flixbro Terrace, Terry Street, Hull. Graduates with a First class degree

BIOGRAPHICAL OUTLINE

	in English Literature.
1968	Dunn receives an Eric Gregory Award for poems later published in *Terry Street*. Moves into new house Marlborough Avenue, Hull.
1969	*Terry Street* published.
1969–71	Assistant Librarian, Brynmor Jones Library, University of Hull, under Philip Larkin.
1970	Wins Scottish Arts Council Book Award for *Terry Street*.
1970	Conservative Party wins the General Election.
1971	Leaves his job at the Brynmor Jones Library and begins freelance writing and review work for magazines including *Encounter*, *London Magazine*, *New Statesman*, *Spectator*, *TLS*.
1972	*The Happier Life* published. Wins Somerset Maugham Award for *Terry Street*. Dunn and Lesley live for several months in the Dordogne region of France in the village of Tursac, near Les Eyzies de Tayac.
1974	*Love or Nothing* published. Edits *A Choice of Byron's Verse*.
1974	Labour, under Harold Wilson, win the October General Election with a majority of three. Eleven Scottish Nationalist MPs elected to Westminster.
1974–5	Fellow in Creative Writing, University of Hull. Teaches classes for the Workers Educational Association, the University of Hull's Extra-Mural Department and Hull College of Art.
1975	Edits *Two Decades of Irish Writing*. Verse play *Experience Hotel* performed at The Humberside Theatre. Screenplay for BBC TV *Early Every Morning*. Wins Scottish Arts Council Book Award for *Love or Nothing*.
1976	James Callaghan becomes Prime Minister.
1976	Wins Geoffrey Faber Memorial Prize for *Love or Nothing*. Edits *What is to be Given: Selected Poems of Delmore Schwartz*. Moves into house at 3 Muirfield Avenue, Westbourne Park, Hull, described as 'The Butterfly House' in *Elegies*.
1977	Screenplay for BBC TV: *Running*. Radio play *Scotsmen by Moonlight* broadcast on BBC Radio Scotland.
1978	Lesley Dunn is diagnosed with cancer.

1979	*Barbarians* published. Edits *The Poetry of Scotland*. Television play *Ploughman's Share* broadcast on BBC1 in the *Play for Today* series.
1979	The 'winter of discontent' characterized by industrial unrest and power cuts.
1979	Home Rule referendum held in Scotland. The result was 51.6% in favour and 48.4% against but turn-out is poor. A late amendment to the Scotland Act had stipulated that a victory would need 40% of the whole electorate. This is not the case so Scotland remains under Westminister rule. The SNP brings down the Labour government with a vote of no confidence.
1979	Election of Conservative government under Margaret Thatcher.
1980	Death of father.
1980	Radio play *Wedderburn's Slave* broadcast on BBC Radio Scotland.
1981	Death of Lesley Balfour Dunn on 13 March.
1981	*St. Kilda's Parliament* published. Begins writing for *Glasgow Herald*. Becomes Fellow of Royal Society of Literature.
1981–2	Writer-in-residence, University of Dundee.
1982	Meets Lesley Bathgate. Wins Hawthornden Prize for *St. Kilda's Parliament*. *Europa's Lover* published. Edits *A Rumoured City: New Poets from Hull* and *To Build A Bridge*.
1983	The Conservatives, under Margaret Thatcher, win a landslide victory for a second term.
1984	The miners' strike led by Arthur Scargill.
1984	Dunn and Lesley move to Tayport, Fife, Scotland. Writer-in-residence, University of New England. Screenplay *Anon's People* broadcast on BBC1 Scotland.
1985	Marries Lesley Bathgate. *Elegies* and first collection of short stories *Secret Villages* published.
1986	Wins Whitbread Poetry Award and Whitbread Book of the Year Award for *Elegies*. *Selected Poems 1964–1983* published. Radio play *The Telescope Garden* broadcast on BBC Radio 3.
1986–9	Writer-in-residence at Duncan of Jordanstone College of Art and Dundee Central Library.

1987	Margaret Thatcher wins third and final term of office.
1987	Birth of Robbie Dunn. Made Honorary Professor, Faculty of Arts and Social Sciences, University of Dundee.
1988	*Northlight* published.
1989	Writer-in-residence, University of St. Andrews. US edition of *New and Selected Poems 1966–1988*. Radio play *Andromache*, a verse translation of Racine's *Andromaque*, broadcast on BBC Radio 3.
1989	Poll Tax introduced in Scotland in April.
1990	In January, Strathclyde Regional Council apply for 250,000 warrants against people refusing to pay Poll Tax.
1990	John Major replaces Margaret Thatcher as leader of Conservative Party and Prime Minister.
1990	Birth of Lillias Dunn. Receives Cholmondley Award. Racine's *Andromache* published. *Poll Tax: The Fiscal Fake* published in Chatto & Windus's *Counterblast* pamphlet series. Edits *The Essential Browning*.
1991	Professor of English, University of St. Andrews. Edits *Scotland: An Anthology*.
1992	Edits *The Faber Book of Twentieth-Century Scottish Poetry*. 'Dressed to Kill' broadcast on BBC 2 in the *Words on Film* series.
1992–4	Serves as a member of the Scottish Arts Council.
1993	*Dante's Drum-kit* published. Director, St Andrews Scottish Studies Institute. Establishes M.Litt in Creative Writing at St Andrews.
1995	Edits *The Oxford Book of Scottish Short Stories*.
1996	Second collection of short stories *Boyfriends and Girlfriends* published.
1996	Stone of Destiny, stolen from Scone by King Edward I of England in 1296, returned to Scotland and installed in Edinburgh Castle.
1997	Labour, led by Tony Blair, win the General Election.
1997	Home Rule referendum in Scotland. 74.3% vote in favour.
1997	Dunn and his second wife separate.
1999	Moves to village of Dairsie, North-East Fife, Scotland.
1999	Election for the first directly elected Scottish Parlia-

	ment. New Parliament meets in May in Edinburgh for first time since 1707. Official opening of Parliament by the Queen in July.
2000	*The Donkey's Ears* and *The Year's Afternoon* published.
2003	*New Selected Poems 1964–1999* published.

Abbreviations and References

WORKS BY DUNN

B	*Barbarians* (London: Faber & Faber, 1979)
DDK	*Dante's Drum-kit* (London: Faber & Faber, 1993)
E	*Elegies* (London: Faber & Faber, 1985)
EL	*Europa's Lover* (Newcastle upon Tyne: Bloodaxe Books, 1983)
LN	*Love or Nothing* (London: Faber & Faber, 1974)
N	*Northlight* (London: Faber & Faber, 1988)
PT	*Poll Tax: The Fiscal Fake* (London: Chatto & Windus, 1990)
SKP	*St. Kilda's Parliament* (London: Faber & Faber, 1981)
SP	*Selected Poems 1964–1983* (London: Faber & Faber, 1986)
TDE	*The Donkey's Ears* (London: Faber & Faber, 2000)
THL	*The Happier Life* (London: Faber & Faber, 1972)
TS	*Terry Street* (London: Faber & Faber, 1969)
TYA	*The Year's Afternoon* (London: Faber & Faber, 2000)

INTERVIEWS WITH DUNN

Crawford	'Douglas Dunn talking with Robert Crawford', *Verse*, 4, (1985), 26–35
PD	'Interview with The Devil: Douglas Dunn', *The Printer's Devil*, A, (1990), 12–34
Dösa	'A Different Drummer: Attila Dösa Interviews Douglas Dunn', *Poetry Review*, Vol 89 No 3, Autumn 1999: 27–34
Haffenden	Haffenden, John, ed., *Viewpoints: Poets in Conversa-*

	tion (London: Faber & Faber, 1981), pp.11–34
O'Donoghue	O'Donoghue, Bernard, 'An Interview with Douglas Dunn', *Oxford Poetry*, 2 2, (Spring 1985), 44–51
Oxley	Oxley, William, 'Interview with Douglas Dunn', *Acumen*, 13, (April 1991), 9–21

OTHER WORKS CITED

BNTS	*Bête Noire*, Terry Street Special Edition, no. 16 (Autumn 1994)
CP	Hardy, Thomas, *Collected Poems* (London: Macmillan, 1968)
King	King, P. R., ed., *Nine Contemporary Poets: a critical introduction* (London: Methuen, 1979)
RDD	Crawford, Robert, and Kinloch, David, eds., *Reading Douglas Dunn* (Edinburgh: Edinburgh University Press, 1992).

Introduction

Douglas Dunn has described himself as 'a lyric poet distracted by social concerns that are not of my invention' (O'Donoghue, 47) and once mocked such distractions by calling himself 'Horace with a view / Of the gasworks' (*THL*, 57). In a career spanning over forty years, Dunn has produced a body of work that, in the words of Scottish critic Cairns Craig, 'has developed [...] through continual inner dialogues: dialogues between styles, between cultures, between possible identities of the poet.'[1] The early suburban nocturne 'Close of Play' begins with an image of cricketers with 'the manners of ghosts, / Wandering in white on the tended ground' but ends in 'a place without manners' where 'The rapists gather under hedges and bridges' (*TS*, 41–2). 'Close of Play' not only implies that life in 'the sweet-smelling suburbs' is merely a question of 'manners' but also offers poetry as a way of questioning what appears to be settled and perfected. It is irresponsible, the poem seems to be saying, for the lyric poet to ignore what distracts him.

Dunn's poetry is inextricable from such ideas of responsibility. In the introduction to his work for Charles King and Iain Crichton Smith's 1986 anthology *Twelve Modern Scottish Poets*, Dunn wrote that 'I am conscious of writing for other people'.[2] When Dunn writes in another early poem 'Men of Terry Street' that 'they are too tired / And bored to look long at comfortably' (*TS*, 17) he is registering the distance between his way of life and theirs. At the same time, he is drawing attention to the fact that there is an unremarked voyeurism involved in this type of social realist poetry that should make both poet and reader uncomfortable. Looking is both a poetical and political practice. Such passages also underline the overtly visual nature of large areas of Dunn's poetry. Neil Corcoran has highlighted the preponderance of dramatizations of observer and observed and usefully defined it as a 'perceptual reciprocity'.[3]

Dunn's poetry, then, insists that looking at things and making them into poems are ideological behaviours. To write poetry is to enter into a genre of pre-existent concerns and modes that may converge not only with dominant political and social wisdoms but also with an array of deep-seated audience expectations. The poet may, as a consequence, find himself adopting or being invited to adopt attitudes he does not share or wish to have. For Dunn, writing poetry is synonymous with guarding against and actively resisting such influences and with not taking things at face value. Dunn's assertion at the start of his poetic career that 'There are many worlds, there are many laws' finds later echoes in 'I see / Plurals and distances' and 'I won't disfigure loveliness I see / With an avoidance of its politics.'[4]

Dunn's perceptual reciprocity and his concern that observation should not equal simplification have important effects. The evocation of 'many worlds' disturbs *Terry Street*'s apparently settled realism and begs questions about the extent of its authenticity *and* its constructedness. As Ian Gregson points out, the line announces a concern that runs through Dunn's œuvre: 'to demonstrate that there is an official world-view – a dominant ideology – which deliberately misses too much out.'[5] So, for example, while it would at first sight be very easy to argue that, like many male poets of his generation, Dunn is seemingly unaware of gender issues, a close reading of the 'Terry Street Poems' reveals a quiet insistence on the central role of women in the life of the street. The only men who are fully realized are old men and the husband of the departing family in 'A Removal from Terry Street'. Similarly, the collective effect of poems such as 'The Clothes Pit', 'Men of Terry Street' and 'Young Women in Rollers' is to evoke gender as a reciprocal economy of looking in which men and women hold each other accountable to cultural norms. Dunn's anxiety about his status in the community is visible in the way he measures himself and feels himself measured against these norms.[6]

In opening the subject of Dunn's relation to gender politics, it is of course important to proceed with caution in case we find ourselves asking a poet to be a more vocal activist or a more rigorous theorist. While it is true that feminism has emerged during Dunn's career, it is also true that he belongs to the generation for whom class remains the primary ground of political struggle. One might also ask whether it is possible for a male poet to choose to write a feminist poem; and, even if this were possible, where the value of such a self-conscious poem would be located and for whom it would be valuable. Dunn himself has observed that,

> Poets are led to their subjects by pressures which are rarely 'theoretical'. I remember reading how Rosa Luxembourg excused the poet Korolenko from political themes saying that the memory of wind in the birch trees was of more significance for him. Perhaps it's important to stress that poetry is almost always benevolent and that 'theory', while intending to be benign, often isn't (at least in a poetic sense) for the reason that theories, by their very nature, involve themselves in forms of special pleading and narrow argument.[7]

It is clear, then, that, for Dunn, care for the 'many worlds' of experience and their 'many laws' derives partly from a conception of poetry's difference from other discourses. Two other sources are especially notable. First, Dunn has stated that he was greatly influenced by a comment from what many would regard as the start of the post-war English mainstream: Robert Conquest's introduction to the 1956 Movement anthology *New Lines*. Dunn has said that he approves of Conquest's assertion that poetry is founded on 'reverence for the real person or event' and interprets this as knowing when to keep quiet.[8] Second, as Sean O'Brien has noted, Dunn's aesthetics and politics are rooted in Scottish traditions 'whose radical conservatism is difficult for an English audience to identify exactly.'[9] Dunn gives a good indication of what this radicalism might mean in an interview given to William Oxley: 'What's important is not politics-in-poetry so much as avoiding the timidity that side-steps political issues' (Oxley, 15–16). Another indication comes in his observation elsewhere that Larkin's values 'were conventional ... but radical in that he actually believed in them without hypocrisy'.[10] The contrast with habitual English attitudes is implicit but telling.

Dunn is certainly in dialogue with what he sees as English complacency and a resultant timidity about aesthetic form, political institutions and the relations between them. He wants to test the apparently perfected forms of poetry and politics. For example, he has remarked that 'British society' does not exist 'except as a notion of the ruling class and the military. How can a society exist when it's not supported by a culture?' (O'Donoghue, 46). In a specifically Scottish context, Dunn also wants to answer the sort of questions Seamus Heaney poses, albeit to a different end, in his 'Squarings' sequence: 'Where does spirit live?' or 'how inhabited the windy light?'[11] Such questions have a particular force and feeling in the context of what Dunn has called 'the Scottish tragedy – that the democratic spirit of Scotland, or, more accurately, its potential, has never had the opportunity to express the people who created it, but has always been in opposition' (Oxley, 17). Dunn's dialogues are concerned to relate the artistic and the political but his reference to 'opposition' does not imply that they lead to 'either / or' choices. The experience of reading Dunn's work is akin to that which Ian Campbell identifies with older writers such as Walter Scott, James Hogg and Robert Louis Stevenson. The effect of their work is

> to change the audience's way of looking at their country ... [and] in many cases the major Scottish author reaches out beyond the Scottish audience to the non-Scot, to educate, to attract, to evoke some kind of calculated response.[12]

Dunn makes clear connections between past failures of the imagination and an unarticulated and untransacted democratic spirit. His work is continually informed not just by a project to recover a national consciousness but by an equally pressing concern to understand what future form this consciousness might take.

Recuperative narratives that seek links between the untransacted past, present reality and future potential of Scotland's democratic spirit suggest that historical continuity is at best paradoxical. In this context, it seems appropriate to ask whether Dunn can be called a post-colonial writer since similar questions preoccupy the emerging literatures described by Salman Rushdie's memorable phrase 'the empire writes back'. We have already noted how Dunn rejects the 'dominant/subdominant' history of England and Scotland. Indeed, to return to Ian Gregson's observation, it is clear that Dunn also sees this history as the product of a dominant ideology that deliberately misses too much out. Similarly, colonial discourse uses binaries that legitimate the precedence of one cultural position over another and it is certainly true that Dunn's poetry continually redraws and remakes apparently settled pairs such as 'civilized / barbarian'. There is also some convergence between Dunn's perceptual reciprocity and postcolonial theory's discussion of what happens when the colonized subject returns the colonizing gaze.

At the same time, Dunn is a First World writer drawing on a very different set of experiences to many practitioners of emerging literatures. Bernard O'Donoghue's observation that Seamus Heaney 'seeks simultaneous connection with and detachment from both the English and Irish traditions' seems equally applicable to Dunn's poetic relationship with England and Scotland.[13] In his 1991 interview with William Oxley, Dunn remarked that 'I don't see any conflict between being a Scot and writing in English' and that it is important to 'discriminate between one kind of Englishness and another' (Oxley, 16, 20). Dunn has also insisted that close attention must be paid to historical facts. He reminded William Oxley that 'Fear of war was what persuaded many Scots in the debates before the Union in 1707' (Oxley, 20). The historian Michael Hechter observes that educated Scots quickly began a process of Anglicization with the result that

> [b]ecause the rulers of the Scottish state were themselves culturally Anglicized, their English counterparts felt it unnecessary to insist upon total control over Scottish cultural institutions as they had done in Wales and Ireland.[14]

Indeed, the Scottish parliament was virtually the only Scottish institution to be abolished by the 1707 Act of Union. These factors contributed to a culturally complex relation between national self-consciousness and nationalism which is clearly evident in Dunn's poetry. It is also worth remembering Scotland's role in the British Empire. Hechter notes that the bulk of nineteenth-century imperial administrators came from either the Home Counties or Lowland Scotland.[15] It is hardly surprising then that, as Dunn has observed, 'Colonialism is an intellectually and emotionally awkward area for Scots.'[16] In this context, Dunn's recreations of historical events and personalities do more than remind both Scottish and English readers that, as Hechter notes, 'English military and political control in the peripheral regions was buttressed by a racist ideology which held that... Anglo-Saxon culture was inherently superior to Celtic'.[17] They also have the effect of restaging debates about, say, engagement and withdrawal or apathy and autonomy which have marked Scottish culture and character. At the same time, poems as superficially diverse as 'Renfrewshire Traveller' (*LN*, 22), 'The Apple Tree' (*SKP*, 16), 'The Dark Crossroads' (*N*, 62) and 'Weeding a Border' (*DDK*, 59) insist that to think oneself Scottish means having to think beyond a predetermined identity in which Scots have often been complicit. The ground of identity has to be continually recontested.

Dunn, then, has always had uncomfortable things to say to England and Scotland and has sought to remind them that their relationship continues to restage and work through its origins in internal colonialism. Similarly, in poems such as 'The Come-on' and 'Glasgow Schoolboys, Running Backwards' he has had equally uncompromising things to say about education and class (*B*, 13–14, 39). When he borrowed the concept of a 'middle generation' from Polish poetry and applied it to post-war British poetry – specifically that published after 1965 – he used it to identify a group of poets including Tony Harrison and Seamus Heaney who had come to maturity with a radically different set of expectations formed in part by the 1944 Education Acts and the rise of the welfare state. Without saying so directly Dunn included himself in that generation whose expectations can be generalized into beliefs that culture means more than elite artistic and literary practices; and that society is synonymous with the amelioration of people's lives. Such beliefs are surely behind his caustic observation that 'the phrase "the English Language" tends to promote a British "national unity" that has never existed.'[18] This sense of the fictionality of national unity is, one suspects, a decisive factor in Dunn's search for vantage points. 'Syndrome' in his second volume, *The Happier Life*, asserts that 'The only answer is to live quietly, miles away' (33). Although Dunn chose not to include the poem in his *Selected Poems*, it does introduce a major theme that W. N. Herbert characterizes as 'the gaining of a perspective in which to view [civilization]' (*RDD*,

124-5). Living quietly, miles away, also suggests the pastoral, but for a poet who rejects political timidity and whose work is nourished by dialogues between apparently exclusive positions, the pastoral answer is not a simple one. Sean O'Brien notes that Dunn's work admits that

> [H]aving it both ways is one of the functions of the pastoral. While the poet may be 'miles away', nursing his pessimism or his garden, his seclusion is indicated by the large tricolour brandished from an upstairs window.[19]

Dunn's response would presumably be that 'having it both ways' is something about which one has no choice.

It is this sense of unresolved and perhaps irresolvable dialogues and negotiations that I will explore in the rest of this study. It has to be said that Dunn's critics have sometimes seemed less comfortable with his dialogues than the poet himself. For example, John Ash attacked *St. Kilda's Parliament* for its lack of 'a unifying imagination' and read its variety of forms and styles as 'the symptom of profound uncertainty'.[20] More recently, Edna Longley complained that *New Selected Poems 1964-1999* contained 'Rather too many poems [...] written on discursive automatic pilot' and that 'Dunn compromises the civic thrust of his work whenever he settles for the occasional poem ("Ode to a Paperclip", verse about libraries or school dinners) instead of waiting for the poem which is itself an occasion.'[21] Such judgments may seem unnecessarily harsh but the variety of Dunn's poetry certainly challenges any attempt at an incremental account of it. The shape of Dunn's career and his identity as a poet will be the principle concerns of this study. I should point out immediately that I will not be discussing Dunn's essays, editorial work, short stories or his radio plays except in passing.[22] I have chosen to focus on his poetry because it contains not only some the finest lyric poetry written in English in the late-twentieth century but also because it engages with a number of matters – how to write political poetry, how to write lyrically *and* discursively – that have preoccupied surprisingly few mainstream British poets. It is here that Dunn's achievement can be measured and judged immensely valuable.

1

Part of a Place

When Douglas Dunn's first collection *Terry Street* appeared in 1969 it seemed clearly identifiable with what Jonathan Raban, writing two years later in *The Society of the Poem*, would term centralism. Centralism, Raban argued, used 'a common, simple voice' to 'construct a notional 'actuality' which paralleled the English reader's everyday 'sociological and political environment'. Poets like John Fuller, Ian Hamilton and Hugo Williams explored 'shared forms of experience – marriage, loneliness, the fear of death, the routine of work' and let into them 'slippery trickles of insight and menace'.[1] Many of *Terry Street*'s poems do function in this way. The beginning of Dunn's poetry career also seemed to ally him closely with centralism. Over half of *Terry Street*'s poems had originally been published in magazines such as *New Statesman*, the *Review* and *The Listener*; and eleven of them had appeared in the first Faber *Poetry Introduction*. More to the point, Dunn's use of unusual and precise negative adjectives like 'unlovely' and 'unrotting' (*TS*, 13, 42) was a clear echo of centralism's dominant voice, Philip Larkin, whose own poetry was similarly characterized by words like 'unfingermarked', 'unrecommended' and 'unspent'.[2] The use of such negatives sends complex signals about both centralism and realism. To call something 'unlovely' instead of 'ugly' is not only to be absolutely clear about its attributes but also to describe the conspicuous lack of a quality that ought to be present. There is perhaps something peculiarly English in the way such usages say something horribly final in what looks like the language of understatement. Such usages may also be distant echoes of the progressively disenchanted pragmatism that dominated English cultural and political life in the late 1960s.

Over thirty-five years later it is, in Sean O'Brien's words, 'hard to view *Terry Street* as simply "realistic"' (*RDD*, 68) or, indeed, to identify it so readily with post-war English poetic centralism. Much of this has to do with Dunn's responsible portrayal of his own ambivalence. He shares a common ground of class with Terry Street's inhabitants but is set apart by his cultural origins and his education. He admires aspects of their lives – uncomplicated masculinity in 'Men of Terry Street' – but is repulsed by their acceptance of materialism and what the book's first poem calls 'the litter of pop rhetoric' (*TS*, 13). This ambivalence is, however, just one manifestation of a wider process. *Terry Street* shows Dunn recognizing cultural constructions and his own role within them, exploring and negotiating their limits and then trying to bring them into a new relationship. Dunn's later writings about the book and comments in interviews reveal an implicit dialogue between England and Scotland that not only works to expose the internal contradictions of both but also opens onto a wider debate about cultural unity and disunity.

Jonathan Raban characterized the centralist poet as 'a revealer, not a maker' but the nature of what is revealed in *Terry Street*'s opening poem shows that Dunn was already a very different sort of poet.[3] 'The Clothes Pit' focuses on the young women of the street and their involvement in a rising consumerism that keeps people in a permanent condition of 'being behind'. The opening and closing stanzas highlight how wider arguments about culture and society emerge from careful observation of material details:

> The young women are obsessed with beauty.
> Their old-fashioned sewing machines rattle in Terry Street.
> *They must keep up, they must keep up.*
> *
> Three girls go down the street with the summer wind.
> The litter of pop rhetoric blows down Terry Street,
> Bounces past their feet, into their lives.
>
> (TS, 13)

References to '*International Times*' and 'the Liverpool Poets', 'pot' and 'pop' locate the poem firmly in the late 1960s. They contribute to the poem's argument by focusing on one of the ways that consumer capitalism ensures people will want to 'keep up', namely by turning rebellion against itself into a commodity and selling it back to them. Dunn's pop culture references suggest that the 'intellectual grooming' the young women supposedly lack is just another dubious commodity. Their real impoverishment is that they only have access to culture's outward forms such as clothes and make-up. And there is a strong sense in which the ending of the poem implies that the young women's 'paradise' is 'inarticulate' because 'pop rhetoric' has both detached them from their native speech and encouraged them to dream in language of symbols that is not their own.

The poem describes the erosion of genuine working-class culture. In an interview given to John Haffenden, Dunn spoke of the lives of Terry Street's residents being controlled by

> pressures which didn't come from our common culture but from other sources. I found that disturbing. I was conscious of writing about that, as in the first poem of the book, and not about Terry Street, but about the country as a whole. (Haffenden, 15)

Dunn's comment about being disturbed highlights that he has yet to develop what might be termed a continually renewable way of looking. At the start of his career he only seems able to record the act and consequences of the working class eagerly putting on what the poem terms the 'lush, impermanent' aspects of consumerism. Words such as 'obsessed', 'teasing' and 'rampant' combine a residual moralizing with a kind of political revulsion. In the same interview Dunn says Terry Street is 'more like a village [...] a little community' and that 'to some extent my expression of Terry Street was a surrogate, a substitute for my commitment to somewhere else' (Haffenden, 14, 16). Part of the reason for Dunn's equivocating portrayal of Terry Street can be located here in his disappointed expectations that the street's and, indeed, Hull's remoteness from the metropolitan centre had somehow imbued it with a way of life similar to his home village of Inchinnan in Renfrewshire:

> I think it could be argued that remote communities manage to sustain an ethic which when contrasted with the priorities of more up to date sophisticated contemporary societies and communities looks increasingly valuable. (Crawford, 26)

Significantly, some of the poems at the end of the Terry Street sequence – 'Young Women in Rollers' and 'A Window Affair' – not only reject the silent looking at 'hard things' (*TS*, 34) and the sense of the poet being literally behind glass that 'The Clothes Pit' introduces but also admit the uselessness of dreaming of 'ideal communities', 'the ideal life', and 'ideals' in general (*TS*, 30, 33, 34). 'The Clothes Pit', then, marks the beginning of a larger implicit argument in which Dunn's vision of the street expands to include not only the erosion of working-class culture and community but also a wider dissolution and confusion. It is a confusion that Dunn has described thus: 'Either Hull was the centre of the imperium, or these people hadn't been beyond its frontiers' (*BNTS*, 8). The impact of 'pop rhetoric' has implications beyond the working class and the North of England. Terry Street and Hull become emblems for everything that England is and everything that Inchinnan and Scotland, in contrast, are not. Dunn has, for example, told Jane Stabler that class consciousness is 'a rotten, rancid and disgusting thing in British society, not native to Scotland until someone put it there' (*RDD*, 1). He has also said that 'A couple of years after leaving Terry Street, I did have an active dislike of Terry Street and all streets like it, and especially the kind of society which allowed such streets to exist' (Haffenden, 19).

The relation between the individual life and worldly institutions is also explored in an implicit argument throughout the sequence about culture. The argument is made through links and contrasts between a distinctive group of words: 'culture', 'pop rhetoric', 'entertainment', 'the [...] Third', 'westerns', 'last year's hits' and 'radios'. Dunn disapproves of how the new 'pop' culture erodes what Raymond Williams had observed in *Culture and Society 1780–1950*, originally published in 1958: 'The basis of a distinction between bourgeois and working-class culture is only secondarily in the field of intellectual and imaginative work [...] The crucial distinction is between alternative ideas of the nature of social relationship.'[4] In the same way, the Terry Street sequence implicitly asks what are a 'culture' and a 'way of life' and what is the relationship between them. What Dunn records is a new, ephemeral culture – which has no connection with anyone's life – coming to stand for a way of life.

The argument becomes more overt as the Terry Street sequence progresses but it also becomes more complicated. The poems begin to move between the largely exterior observation of 'The Clothes Pit' and a subtly nuanced intersubjectivity that begins, quite abruptly, in the closing stanza of the second poem of the sequence 'New Light on Terry Street' (*TS*, 14): 'Yet there is no unrest. The dust is so fine. / You hardly notice you have grown too old to cry out for change.' The poem seems a straightforward celebration of the 'First sunshine for three weeks' but, like 'The Clothes Pit', introduces many elements of what John Osborne terms 'Dunn's discontinuous critique of his Terry Street neighbours'. It is a critique that includes, says Osborne,

> political quietism; an erosion of family values one symptom of which is the abandonment of the grandparental generation; a passive consumption of pop music, T.V. and radio; a low valuation of education, knowledge or the arts; drunkenness; an environmental blindness characterized by endemic littering; and an archaic sexual economy ... (*BNTS*, 93)

Reading this back into the poem makes its final 'You' extremely ambiguous. At a simple level, it can be read as Dunn acknowledging the common ground of class and locating himself in the community where he lives. Dunn addresses and includes himself in the scene and thereby suggests its inner life. The 'You' also addresses the reader and asks her to consider that the forces that sap the energies of the working class are at work throughout society as a whole.

The nascent intersubjectivity of 'New Light on Terry Street' is developed in 'The Terry Street Fusiliers' (*TS*, 19) which pictures one of Terry Street's old men limping down the street, 'with a stick much faster than I walk. / If Terry Street was attacked, he would defend us'. The poet is now a part of 'us' but the odd anti-climax of the last line – 'I must walk straighter, lose a little weight' – suggests he recognizes that to recover a class identity is to recover things one may not want. The closing phrase 'lose a little weight' is perhaps required to do too much work. It is as if it is literally meant to disperse the weight of sentimental feeling accumulated in the poem – a sentimentality Dunn censures throughout the sequence – *and*, in its cool detachment, to add 'weight' to Dunn's portrayal of belonging. The poem also mounts a discrete but telling response to nation and empire. In one sense, the poem's title is a bitterly ironic reference to the militaristic drives of nationalism and the way the working class has been used and discarded by nationalist and imperialist dreams. The poem also implies that the working class's political quietism – referred to obliquely in 'Yet there is no unrest' in 'New Light on Terry Street' – has allowed this to happen.

Dunn is presenting us with a form of life whose own values are identified in terms of discourses and structures inimical to itself. As with his disapproving remarks about pop culture, such a view contributes to a wider argument arising from his disappointed expectations about community. Dunn's expectations are made clearer by later remarks in an interview with Robert Crawford about the ethics of 'remote communities' looking 'increasingly valuable ... when contrasted with the priorities of more up to date sophisticated contemporary societies'. Indeed, he goes on to refer to some communities' 'aggressive ... evaluation of their own decency' (Crawford, 26). However, the Terry Street sequence makes equally clear that Dunn is not prepared to ignore contradictions between what he believes and what he sees. As we have already noted, several poems in the sequence do not merely contrast the local with the national. The local has a form of life that is different from the national and its totalizing narratives but these forms of life are at once mutually inimical *and* mutually supportive. Dunn's Scottish origins mean he comes to Terry Street with the expectation that its community, while vulnerable to the workings of nation, will not be passive and politically quietist. The fact that these are the very things he is forced to record prompt his reading of Terry Street as 'the country as a whole' i.e. England. It is a national identity that Dunn would later confidently describe from the vantage point of the Firth of Tay in 'Here and There' as a self-deluding 'Albionic pride' which blinds the English nationalist to the fact that he himself is now 'the provincial, an undignified / Anachronism' (*N*, 28–9). In the immediate context of the Terry Street sequence, however, Dunn's poetry describes the difficulty of reading England accurately from the inside. If Hull is either at the centre or nowhere then one could presumably say the same about other parts of the country. The result is that it becomes impossible to make the sort of reading of place that Dunn describes to Robert Crawford: 'The appearance of a countryside dramatizes so much about changes in life, livelihood, and it suggests what's permanent about what people do, and those things which are temporary' (Crawford, 27). The fact that such a reading cannot easily be made perhaps leads to the later conclusion that 'British society' does not actually exist. Again, this contrasts markedly with Scotland where, in Dunn's view, one is always precisely located: 'You've got to remember that a good deal of the population in Scotland lives in small towns or villages' (PD, 30).

The intersubjectivity of these early poems in the sequence shows Dunn starting to rethink traditional oppositions. It also has more directly poetic consequences. Writing in P. R. King's *Nine Contemporary Poets*, Dunn referred to metre as 'too much of an instrument for the exclusion of uncertainty' and goes on to say of 'A Removal From Terry Street' (*TS*, 20) – with its famous last line 'That man, I wish him well. I wish him grass' – that

> it was the weight of observation and narrative and the presence of people and objects – 'Four paperback westerns' and 'Two whistling youths' – which made it unnatural or undesirable to sustain the iambic rhythm of the classic English line throughout.' (King, 224)

In fact, the poem contains only two exact pentameters in lines seven and eleven. The comparative rarity of such lines in contemporary English poetry returns our attention to the rest of the poem. Indeed, 'Whose mischief we are glad to see removed' does not sound contemporary at all: Dunn is self-consciously writing blank verse. The other lines' shorter sentences, enjambments and nine or eleven syllables mime the seemingly casual nature of the removal but they also continually invoke 'the iambic rhythm of the classic English line'. In terms of the English canon, blank verse signals the bestowal of both quality of attention and status. For example, Malvolio's final speech in *Twelfth Night*, in which he acquires a wounded dignity, is the only one given him in blank verse. In contrast, Falstaff's final speeches in *Henry IV Part II* are in prose and Prince John's comments that he and his followers 'are banished till their conversations / Appear more wise and modest to the world' underline what is meant by Shakespeare's verse / prose distinction between upper and lower class characters. The destination of the family of the poem is not revealed but we might assume from a later poem in the sequence that Dunn is observing children of Terry Street residents moving to one of 'the new estates' mentioned in 'The Patricians'. If this assumption is correct then Dunn's characters in 'A Removal ...' are moving from dispossession to possession. Dunn's decision not to 'sustain' blank verse throughout perhaps registers both this transition and a recognition that responsibility to 'the lives of other people' will always exceed poetic form.

The poem also highlights how Dunn's early titles usually sound like Victorian genre paintings and how each poem, in its own way, presents us with a problematic realism. In some poems this stems from an exploration of the limiting politics of vision involved in some poetic practices but in 'A Removal ...' this work is done by the poem's famous last line. In the introduction to his work written for P. R. King's anthology, Dunn stated that

> [t]he last line of the poem is intended as ironic [...] as an image of vanity, of that man's touching faith in progress, and of my own unjustifiable cynicism in an environment which perfectly embodied the shame and wormwood of British society.
>
> (King, 224)

Whether or not Dunn's cynicism is unjustifiable the last line of 'A Removal From Terry Street' highlights an important aspect of Dunn's early poetry which Ian Gregson usefully terms 'ruined lyricism' (*RDD*, 29). What seems clear is that Dunn's lyricism is 'ruined' because it carries within it the expectation of location within both a particular place and a particular community. This expectation is frustrated by the facts and pressures of urban living in the late twentieth century and by the wider political and social landscape of England. Most importantly, though, if the poem's last line is read as early evidence of a 'ruined lyricism', which is itself founded in disappointed expectations of place and community, then it also demands to be read as an oblique example of how Scotland functions as an ever present structure of feeling. Dunn has described this structure to Jane Stabler as 'my interior Third World, a different time zone' (*RDD*, 4). The irony and cynicism of Dunn's wishes for the man with the lawnmower inscribe a contrast between England and Scotland, between displacement and rootedness. The man who does not have grass is unable to respond to place and landscape in such a way as to make his life there contribute to the drama of the 'permanent' and the 'temporary'.

Intersubjectivity is at its most sophisticated in the three key poems at the end of the Terry Street sequence, 'Young Women in Rollers', 'The Silences' and 'A Window Affair' (*TS*, 29–30, 32, 33–4). In the first of these, young women visiting a married friend are initially presented with the cool objectivity of the opening poems of the sequence. The terms used in this presentation – 'last year's fashions', singing 'words softly to the new tunes', 'With nothing to do but talk of what it is to love' – portray the young women as largely passive participants in structures of capitalist desire. Suddenly, in marked contrast to the rest of the sequence, the observing poet is visible:

> This time they see me at my window, among books,
> A specimen under glass, being protected,
> And laugh at me watching them.
> They minuet to Mozart playing loudly
>
> On the afternoon Third. They mock me thus,
> They mime my softness.
>
> (*TS*, 29)

Dunn's initial reaction is to congratulate himself on his 'softness' and to contrast his books and Mozart with the fact that 'The slum rent-masters are at one with Pop' but the next stanza dissolves the poem into something more elusive and surreal. The women's legs become disembodied, the return of Dunn's look undermines his role as unseen, all-seeing narrator and the whole poem pauses, 'floating' like the women's legs and the soot in the afternoon air. When it regains momentum – 'They disappear into the house' – its viewpoint has been changed irrevocably. Dunn has realized the limits of the cultural formation he sits in and the image of 'a specimen under glass' takes on a wider cultural implication:

> I want to be touched by them, know their lives,
> Dance in my own style, learn something new.
> At night, I even dream of ideal communities.
> Why do they live where they live, the rich and the poor?

> Tonight, when their hair is ready, after tea,
> They'll slip through the legs of policemen.
> I won't be there, I'll be reading books elsewhere.
> There are many worlds, there are many laws.

The question about rich and poor seems naïve but it points to an answer: that the divisions of rich and poor are reinforced by culture and that each group is equally a specimen to the other. For a moment, the young women suggest another possibility for their ability to 'dance in [their] own style' gives them a freedom Dunn cannot possess. The conflicts and apparent contradictions of culture can also be sites of interaction where 'something new' can be learnt and, in this perspective, Dunn's dream of ideal communities is not wholly ironic. The stanza of floating legs and soot suggests that neither the world of books and Mozart nor the world of 'Pop' have more or less value than each other. The moment of the returned look places them, as it does Dunn and the women, in a transformative relation to each other. It is the poem's recognition of this potential that allows the young women to 'slip through' laws which are as surely the laws of realism as they are those of the supposedly liberal state.[5] The line 'I want to be touched by them, know their lives' yearns for involvement in the everyday life of the working class out of which the poet has been translated. The speaker of the poem is also situated between the life of the street and the English idea of high culture represented by 'the Third'. As an educated, working-class Scot he feels kinship with both but cannot hope for membership of either.

However, if 'Young Women in Rollers' holds out the possibility of culture as a place of transformative relations then 'The Silences' abruptly dashes it. In the interview given to John Haffenden, Dunn commented that this poem 'says most about [...] the country as a whole' (15–16). The inarticulacy portrayed in the earlier poems resulted from cultural hegemony and is a symptom of something that is at once more fundamental and more pervasive:

> They are a part of the silence of places,
> The people who live here, working, falling asleep,
> In a place removed one style in time outwith
> The trend of places. They are like a lost tribe.

(*TS*, 32)

The use of the Scots word 'outwith' instead of the English 'outside' or 'beyond' resists easy incorporation into the text and, by extension, into the wider context of English literature. It reveals the limits of the world-view such literature expresses.

Questions naturally arise about the nature of the apparently generalized 'silence of places' and its origins. The phrase 'the trend of places' alludes obliquely to the way urban spaces are structured by capitalist desire at the same time as it emphasizes the remoteness of 'here'. The poem's earlier 'These are edges round a quiet centre where lives are lived' seems to offer a straightforward argument about centre and margins. However, 'They are like a lost tribe' suggests something more unsettling: that a whole stratum of society lives in a state that is so marginal it functions as a species of absence. This recalls the description of Hull that ends an earlier poem in the sequence 'Sunday Morning Among The Houses Of Terry Street': 'A city of disuse, a sink, a place, / Without people it would be like the sea-bottom' (*TS*, 24). This picture of a peripheral English city contrasts sharply with Dunn's comments on Scotland and the 'increasingly valuable' ethics of its 'remote communities' (Crawford, 26).

'A Window Affair' (*TS*, 33-4) at first sight draws a dispirited, even pessimistic, conclusion: 'There is a house I feel I have to leave, / Because my life is cracked [...]'. However, we should beware of taking this self-dramatization at face value. The body of the poem emphasizes 'looking', 'glass', 'the love of eyes and silence' and, perhaps most tellingly, 'I grasp only the hard things, windows, contempts'. This portrayal of the gap between observer and observed, subject and object – which the sequence has made some effort to bridge through experiments with intersubjectivity – is pessimistic about the compositional strategy of the sequence as a whole. Careful, responsible looking at the life of the street has shown not only that looking in itself may not be enough but that looking is fundamentally problematic. Similarly, while such looking has revealed British society as a place of confusion and division it has done so in a way that has unsettled some of Dunn's most cherished assumptions about class, community and place. Furthermore, the problematics of looking and the politics of vision have unsettled Dunn's own position in both the culture and society that permit Terry Street and streets like it to exist. The Terry

Street sequence shows Dunn coming to terms with the fact that realism, the condition of the working class and English society in general are too complex to be seen in terms of traditional oppositions. The sequence makes plain that the technological revolution had succeeded only in exposing more people to the 'pop rhetoric' of consumer capitalism. The socialist dreams of the 1960s paradoxically began the destruction of the working-class form of life that they sprang from in the first place.

Scotland as an answering, alternative form of life becomes explicit in one of the key poems of Part II of *Terry Street*, 'Landscape With One Figure' (*TS*, 55). The scene is the banks of the River Clyde and its shipyards where 'cranes have come down again / To drink at the river.' Although the 'departing emigrants' of the third stanza suggest a post-industrial landscape, the poem focuses on the presentation of landscape and place as the record of the temporary and permanent aspects of individuals' lives. All parts of the scene are carefully interrelated: the cranes 'speak' to their reflections in the Clyde and are beckoned in turn by the fields, trees, grasses and gulls. In this non-human society of animate and inanimate, there is room for the human too:

> If I could sleep standing, I would wait here
> For ever, become a landmark, something fixed
> For tug crews or seabound passengers to point at,
> An example of being part of a place.

The matter-of-factness of the assertion holds the attention and leads the reader to consider the impossibility of such belonging in the England of Part I of the book. Scotland is presented as the ground of interrelation and accommodation.

Terry Street's penultimate poem 'A Poem in Praise of the British' (60–1) appears to share in what Blake Morrison identifies in Larkin as 'post-imperial tristesse'.[6] However, while Dunn was consciously influenced by Larkin he did not share his politics.[7] Larkin's poetry typically enacts the necessity of making do with the largely unsatisfactory consolations of what Neil Corcoran characterizes as 'the religion of an enduring Englishness'[8]. Dunn's poem, in contrast, deconstructs that whole structure of feeling and mocks any view of England and Englishness as a species of postlapsarian narrative. British power and glory were founded on 'the wish to be inert' and 'the weakness after Empire' is so 'sweet' because it is, in effect, more of the same: 'In this old country, we are falling asleep, under clouds / That are like wide-brimmed hats. This is just right.' The last phrase mimics complicity and thereby satirizes Britain's self-congratulatory enjoyment of the very condition it complains about. If sleep is not the end of empire but its continuation then Dunn's poem makes a wider point about Britain's detachment from its own history.

A detailed analysis of *Terry Street* reveals, then, how closely Dunn's emergent poetic practice is bound up with ideas of nation and its narration. 'A Poem in Praise of the British' is underwritten by an understanding of the connections between home and empire, 'the dainty tea cup and the black gun'. The life of nation may seem largely unexpressed in the life of Terry Street but Dunn's responsible looking leads him to a recognition that the material facts of everyday life are the consequences of larger cultural and social forces. His attempts at understanding the workings of these forces lead him to experiments in intersubjectivity.

What criticism there is on Dunn notes the increasing emphasis on Scottish subjects and perspectives after his relocation to Scotland in the 1980s. However, we should note that in 1979 Dunn wrote that

> [o]ver the years my writing has tried to keep a promise with a Scottish, rural working-class background. It is a promise I don't remember making. What the precise nature of that promise is I don't know. I am certain it is more than a social or political gambit; and I am sure it means more to me than an act of sentimental fidelity. Nor is it an example of one of those manic, wished-for but impossible returns of an uprooted Scotsman. To persevere with the art of poetry is to pick up a bet you make with yourself. Nationality and background are involved in the bet I made.
>
> (King, 221)

In a special issue of *Bête Noire* devoted to *Terry Street* Dunn writes of the working-class people of Hull 'They differed from their Scottish counterparts in holding education in a relatively low regard' (*BNTS*, 7). For Dunn, Scotland and Scottishness are always in a superior relation to England even when they are not overtly present. Scotland is always a defining structure of feeling.

2

Realisms, Rhapsodies and Responsibilities

Douglas Dunn's career was flourishing by the time his second volume *The Happier Life* was published in 1972. He had left his job at the Brynmor Jones Library at the University of Hull and was working as a full-time writer. His poems and reviews appeared regularly in major magazines. *Terry Street* had been awarded the Somerset Maugham Award and his work had appeared in a number of anthologies including Norman MacCaig and Alexander Scott's *Contemporary Scottish Verse 1959–1969*, Dannie Abse's *Corgi Modern Poets in Focus – 1* and Jeremy Robson's *The Young British Poets*. However, far from being seen as a consolidation of early success, *The Happier Life* was a book that displeased critics and has continued to do so. In the interview given to John Haffenden, Dunn observed that 'Reviewers felt that I was setting off on a different tack, trying to write a book that was self-consciously different' and adds that 'I don't think that was the case' (Haffenden, 20). Writing in 1975, Maurice Lindsay used the image of 'The Terry Street Room-at-the-Top Dunn' becoming 'Life-at-the-Top Dunn' to characterize what he saw as the book's greater detachment from its working-class subjects. Sixteen years after the book's publication, Alan Robinson castigated Dunn for 'superficial prejudice' and 'paternalistic complacency' and for turning 'drop-outs into scapegoats'.[1]

It is clear that critics were expecting and have continued to expect *The Happier Life* to be *Return to Terry Street* and that, despite Dunn's insistence to the contrary, his second book *is* very different. In *Terry Street* his original idea had been to mix the poems of parts one and two together but Philip Larkin dissuaded him.[2] *The Happier Life* lacks such clear groupings of poems and its diversity is therefore highly visible. Dunn told Haffenden that there are a number of poems that are 'rather similar to *Terry Street*, but they're too general to be set in Terry Street. There's a seam of these running through the book' (Haffenden, 20–1). At the same time, there are also seams of poems about France and Scotland and a group of long discursive poems of 50 – 124 lines. However, in contrast to the more acerbic critics of *The Happier Life*, it is important to understand its differences to *Terry Street* in poetical *and* ideological terms. In this context, a passage from the Haffenden interview is worth quoting at length. Dunn expresses a wish that

> I could just simply relax and deal with the play of phenomena and experience in my imagination [...] rather than be concerned with subjects which – on the surface at least – are recognizably social. There are times too when I've thought I'd work through these subjects in the hope of getting rid of them, working them out of my system, so that I could start to become a different kind of poet [...]. But the way in which I end up writing some poems is by the *via negativa*, which to me seems the only appropriate way of dramatizing my testimony. To do it from purely lyric motives [...] is to me dishonest, and evasive, when I have other things on my mind which I'm condemned to remember. I would like to work towards the position where it wouldn't be, but I realize that there would have to be changes in society and the whole foundation on which our society is based before that could happen.
>
> (Haffenden, 23)

This refusal of dishonesty may partly account for *The Happier Life*'s greater use of Larkinesque negatives such as 'unfactual', 'unmissed', 'unkept', 'unbothered' and 'untended'. There is more than twice the number than in *Terry Street*. Bernard O'Donoghue has also noted that many poems end with phrases such as 'live in dirt', 'nothing will change' and 'there is nothing new' (*RDD*, 40). Equally notable are the eight poems that use images of silence to convey dispossession or impermanence. The 'rented silence' of 'Modern Love' (*THL*, 51) seems to preclude genuine privacy and intimacy just as 'the silence after entertainment' in 'Saturday Night Function' portrays a return to a humdrum death-in-life (*THL*, 55–7). It would be tempting to read all this as a reflection of a wider despondency at the start of the decade that two commentators have characterized as 'a period of "unillusion"'.³ The 1970s did indeed begin with uncertainty and unrest. Edward Heath's Conservative Government presided over steady and seemingly unstoppable increases in property prices, unemployment and inflation. The first two years of the decade saw more strikes and stoppages than at any time since 1926. However, literary uncertainties paralleled economic and political ones. Novelist-critics like David Lodge and Malcolm Bradbury questioned whether realistic imitation and its identification with liberal humanism were appropriate or sustainable.⁴ In poetry, the dominance of both centralism derived from the Movement and the fatalistic lyrics of emotional containment associated with Ian Hamilton and *the Review* suddenly seemed much more precarious. Three of the most important collections of the period – Ted Hughes's *Crow* (1970), Geoffrey Hill's *Mercian Hymns* (1971) and Seamus Heaney's *Wintering Out* (1972) – ask readers to identify with *and* identify the present in varieties of historic and mythic brutality, opportunism, and violence. Images of maiming and mutilation (Hill), dispersed and disintegrated body parts (Hughes) and murder, physical infection and decay (Heaney) evoke exposed and subjugated individual bodies and thereby suggest despair about any possibility of collective forms of cultural and political life.

It's hardly surprising, then, that *The Happier Life* seems much less settled than its predecessor. The responsible looking and careful notations of *Terry Street* could be said to converge with liberal humanism's gentle progressivism. As Dunn remarked to John Haffenden it was not only that 'everything was there to be seen [...] and recommended itself to me in the form of a poem' but also that he was conscious of writing 'about the country as a whole' (Haffenden, 16, 15). Seeing things clearly seemed synonymous with understanding how they might be improved. The earlier book's subtle movements between an observing 'I' and an inclusive 'you' and 'we' seemed to invite readers and residents to be involved in some collective work of transformation. The new book's first poem 'The Garden' signals a separation: 'Neighbours hate it, and know us by it. / We do not mind at all. We rather like it' (*THL*, 11). Its form – thirteen four-line stanzas in fairly close orbit around a ten syllable line – signals a retreat from the often very short free verse of Dunn's debut. The poem ends 'Though this might look neglected, it might grow' which might be as much about formal poetry as about gardens or nations.

Doubts about realism are most explicit in 'The Hunched' with its well-known opening 'They will not leave me, the lives of other people. / I wear them near my eyes like spectacles' (*THL*, 38). The middle of the poem asks similar questions to 'Why do they live where they live, the rich and the poor?' in 'Young Women in Rollers' (*TS*, 29-30) with its 'What makes them laugh, who lives with them?' but its ending is in contrast abrupt and dismissive: 'And not one of them has anything at all to do with me.' In a sense this is literally true but it can also be read as frustration with the poetry perfected in *Terry Street* and its assumptions that there was some useful work to be done – for poet and reader – by making poetry out of 'the lives of other people'. If those lives have nothing to do with the poet then that may also signal a questioning of exactly whose experience the observing 'I' is grounding and to what end.

Frustration becomes explicit rejection in 'Midweek Matinée' which, having portrayed afternoon drunks in some detail, ends 'You claim the right to be miserable / And I can't stand what you bring out into the open' (*THL*, 35-6). Similarly, in 'Under The Stone', 'the tribes of second-hand' are 'our nightmares / Or longings for squalor, the bad meanings we are' (*THL*, 53). What the collection's title poem calls 'the happier life, the uncompetitive' is

> not found among the streets
> Where broken lives and other men's defeats
> Blow with the litter that encamps like squatters
> Up sheltered alleys in old business quarters

(*THL*, 45)

The Happier Life conveys a powerful sense of the urban scene as a place of loss that can only be temporarily alleviated by entertainment or love. The fact that the 'silent places' in 'Backwaters' (*THL*, 21-2) are 'like the bad days in our lives' combines with 'our nightmares' in 'The Hunched' to suggest whatever life we can construct for ourselves in such a place is precarious. In the words of 'The River Through The City', the city is at best a 'bad carnival' (*THL*, 13). *The Happier Life*'s urban poems are populated by distinct groups – 'sullen magnates', 'scholars', 'the saintly, safe-breakers and lovers' – who appear to live in mutual ignorance. This seems to confirm the title poem's assertion that 'Society's a sham [...] / Fragmented into class and sheltered clique' (*THL*, 43). Social atomization is further underlined by the poor in 'Under The Stone' who 'mean nothing'; by the housewives in 'At a Yorkshire Bus-stop' who are 'nothing to do [...] with what's new'; and by the prostitutes in 'Leisure No End' whose 'futures are only personal, / Nothing to do with us' (*THL*, 53, 16, 23).

The title of Dunn's second volume may seem bitterly ironic and many of its poems overwhelmingly negative but there are points of pleasure and interest. These are to be found in different places than in *Terry Street*. In his first collection Dunn explored a productive relationship between precise realist observation and often mysteriously evocative moments which is best explained by his comments on Larkin's style in an interview given to William Oxley in 1991:

> One minute he's talking about an awful pie, and the next he walks along a railway platform in Sheffield and sees 'the ranged / Joining and parting lines reflect a strong / Unhindered moon' [...] It's this idea of lyricism being *earned* that should attract our attention ... it's that swift transition from something as banal as a bad pie to the moon that in its eccentric, unnerving way, guarantees Larkin's lyricism as true. (Oxley, 10)

In this context, the careful notations of 'On Roofs of Terry Street' guarantee the poem's last line where a builder's 'trowel catches the light and becomes precious' (*TS*, 21). In *The Happier Life* such moments are few and far between and what lyricism there is becomes either personal or fictive. An account of aspects of Dunn's youth 'The Friendship of Young Poets' contrasts its past reality – 'My youth was as private / As the bank at midnight' – with imaginings about other people's present lives: 'and from the oars / Drop scales of perfect river like melting glass' (*THL*, 14). 'Five Years Married' begins with the haunting lines 'We have been waltzing in the foggy meadows / At the edges of cliffs, in outmoded evening dress' (*THL*, 46). Similarly, one of the best-known poems from the volume 'The Musical Orchard' and its evocation of 'Those French tunes on the saxophone, / The music inside fruit' (*THL*, 20) verges on the surreal.

If the link between the banal and the lyric has been broken then what replaces it is what might be termed a civil discursiveness. Civil is meant here in its original senses of the relations of citizens with each other and with the body politic; and of what is shared by individuals living and participating in a community. Large parts of *The Happier Life* may display a lack of faith in the transformative potential of realism but elsewhere the volume shows Dunn refusing to be, as he put it to John Haffenden, 'dishonest, and evasive' about 'other things on my mind which I'm condemned to remember' (Haffenden, 23). The result is that poems like 'The Garden', 'Syndrome', 'At a Yorkshire Bus-stop', 'Fixed' and the title poem evoke either the contemplative formalities of Marvell or the satires of Dryden and Pope. However, it is typical of *The Happier Life* in general that these poems are as unsettled as its realist observations. 'The Happier Life' is perhaps the bleakest of the volume's civil poems and reads as a less-deceived farewell to *Terry Street's* 'dream of ideal communities'. The contemporary urban scene in London and the provinces, the 'standard pastoral', 'the easeful place [...] A city where all needs are taken care of / By good men oozing with official love', 'the landscapes of Romance' – all are mapped and found wanting or vulnerable to 'mistakes, disaster, rotten circumstance' (*THL*, 43).

'Fixed' (*THL*, 64-7) is among the most interesting of the civil discursive poems because it highlights another seam in *The Happier Life*: Scotland. Here 'the pastoral side / Of the tall, shipyarded Clyde' is 'a perfect place' and, like 'The Garden', the poem features miniature glades. It is typical of Dunn that he goes on to describe a disappointed return to what might be 'the fabric of a lie' but then asserts that 'Yet there is a rightness in my lies'. The poem ends with Scotland 'Forever there distortedly, / The fixed and visionary part of me.' Scotland and Scottish childhood are also present in 'After The War' and 'Guerillas' (*THL*, 49, 52). 'After The War' is a childhood reminiscence of soldiers in peacetime and children's war games. The poem focuses on one boy – 'one of us' – who leaves the games:

> I heard him on the road
> Running to his mother's house. They lived alone,
> Behind a hedge round an untended garden
> Filled with broken toys, abrasive loss;

This is a subtle and powerful moment of imaginative sympathy that perfectly demonstrates Dunn's belief in 'reverence for the real person or event'.[5] 'Guerrillas' portrays a kind of children's class war through conflict between the sons of wealthy farmers and a narrating 'we' who

> plundered all we envied and had not got,
> As if the disinherited from farther back
> Came to our blood like a knife to the hand.

The poem's language of 'ownership', 'owned', 'envied' and 'disinherited' introduces a theme and a mode that would become prominent in later collections. The disaffected realist commentator and the poet-philosopher torn between tending his 'oppositional horticulture' or firing off salvoes of satirical couplets would be replaced by adopting the persona of people whose lives, in the words of 'Under The Stone', 'mean nothing'. If the civil discursiveness of many of *The Happier Life*'s longer poems often seems to risk a slightly anxious garrulity about how to answer questions like 'Why do they live where they live, the rich and the poor?' without realist imitation then 'Guerrillas' suggests a way forward through dramatizing how the self is written by and writes back to history.

The dissatisfactions and uncertainties evidenced in *The Happier Life* are confirmed by Dunn's decision to reprint less than half its thirty-nine poems in his *Selected Poems 1964–1983*. The sense of the poet feeling his way forward after *Terry Street* is also confirmed by the fact that between 1971 and 1974 he published around fifty poems in magazines – more than enough for a whole new collection – which haven't been reprinted either. Dunn's third collection, *Love or Nothing*, published in 1974, seems much more assured than its predecessor and contemporary reviewers greeted it enthusiastically. Lyman Andrews, writing in the *Sunday Times*, made the oft-quoted assertion that 'With this collection Mr. Dunn steps into the ranks of England's major living poets' and drew attention to the book's greater formalism. Peter Porter in *The Observer* came closer to catching the book's character:

> Dunn can be a neat and efficient reporter, a moving recorder of his Clydeside childhood and a sophisticated New York fabulist, but he

can also startle the reader with completely original juxtapositions and strange rhetorical flights from commonplace material.[6]

The first poem of *Love or Nothing* seems to announce a definite new direction. 'Little Rich Rhapsody' begins 'For he has spent the summer in hotels / Of eight resorts' (*LN*, 7). Bernard O'Donoghue has drawn attention to 'For': 'What does this 'For' resolve? What special knowledge is implied as the previous stage in its argument?' (*RDD*, 40). These questions are more urgent and unsettling because they have to be asked in the context of a short story about an unnamed third person. The opening poems of Dunn's first two collections, 'The Clothes Pit' and 'The Garden', had located the poet and explored what resulted from such precise location. 'Little Rich Rhapsody' partly unsettles us because it starts in the middle of someone else's story. It is also uncomfortable because it is a loose sonnet which deals not with love but adultery and 'all those / Who stop at nothing and who thrill us / With rapid spendings, dissolutions'. More to the point, in the context of *The Happier Life*, the poem also surprises us because that 'For' writes us, so to speak, into the middle of the poet's own new found confidence about what he can and wants to do. It is as if the poem says 'imagination first, reportage second'.

The 'strange rhetorical flights' Porter identified and a desire to put imagination first are clearly present in a new linguistic register. The first third of *Love or Nothing* is full of Latinate and polysyllabic words: 'enshrinements', 'thalassocracies', 'everlastingness', 'expeditionary', 'cartographical morass', 'lustral', 'periplum', 'remembrances' and 'uncherishable'. As that last word indicates, Larkinesque negatives are also highly audible in the first third of the book: 'waiters stamp untipped', sailors waiting for a job are 'unshipped' and 'sit like unstrung banjos', the 'unrescuable grey-drenched browns / of unpruned apple trees'. Words like 'untipped' and 'unrescuable' push such language beyond what's reasonable and, indeed, the first third of *Love or Nothing* does seem to revel in excess.

The sense of a new direction is confirmed by the next three poems: 'The House Next Door', 'Winter Graveyard' and 'Winter Orchard' (*LN*, 8–9, 10–12, 13–14). The first of these is a self-conscious fiction but the second two are more interesting in their explorations of how to combine the report, record and strange rhetoric Porter identified. 'Winter Graveyard' takes a lengthy tour of an overgrown Victorian cemetery and begins with a stanza that is overwhelmingly less-deceived: the cemetery is a 'dead place' of 'uncherishable headstones' and 'unremarkable civilians' with 'no inheritance' whose 'utterly negative remains' are 'lost anatomies'. After twenty-six lines in this vein, the poem begins an extended discussion of 'that era of grand proprieties' which focuses on the 'blue citizenry' whose children died in World War 1. From this point on it is as if the language is unable to bear the weight of a genuine political anger. Lines like 'aspirations of beauty and love / Disregarding corroded vulgarity / And farcical monuments / To sanctities not worth the enshrinement' enact a clogged discursiveness. The last line is therefore all the more remarkable: 'And a white bird leaves a bare tree'. It is a moment of release that is also an instance of the earned lyricism Dunn identifies in Larkin. 'Winter Orchard', in contrast, has these conflicting elements in much better balance. A line like 'The City of what-suburbanly-managerial-God' is deliberately clumsy as if Dunn is mocking his own propensity to lapse into rather grumpy moralizing. It is in the middle of the poem that Dunn's post-*Terry Street* voice emerges:

> It flourished but came to nothing.
>
> Best efforts are negative,
> Seriously beautiful like art.
> Clear light speaks valediction;
> Sparse branches
> In an orchard of goodbyes.

The subject of the first line is an apple and the following lines demonstrate in miniature key elements of Dunn's mature style. The plain but careful description of the fruit becomes the starting point for meditation and reflection. The opening three lines of the verse might be Dunn translating Horace or Virgil or updating Marvell. The closing two are in a similar vein to 'The music inside fruit' – this is language that can only mean poetically. Dunn's deft elision is in a sense his own 'best effort', a demonstration of his conviction that the modes are inevitably and inextricably related.

'Winter Orchard', like 'Winter Graveyard', also involves the dead: the fog becomes an evocation of 'generation upon labouring generation'. Indeed, it would be more correct to say that both poems deal with the historical undead and, in this sense, set the scene for much of what happens in the rest of the volume. *Love or Nothing* contains a number of poems in which Dunn negotiates the weight of history while at the same time accepting that poetry is not a consolation against or escape from history. Poems such as 'Realisms', 'White Fields', 'Renfrewshire Traveller' and 'Clydesiders' explore how the self is located in history (*LN*, 19–21, 32, 22, 37). By doing so, they attempt to answer what Sean O'Brien has characterized as 'the question of where a political poetry was to come *from*' (*RDD*, 72) [Original emphasis]. 'Realisms' – dedicated to the Irish poet Derek Mahon and using his characteristic short-lined tercet – is an uncomfortable combination of Dunn detailing both the kind of political poetry he won't write *and* stating the attractions and rejection of the lyric dishonesty and evasion he would later describe to John Haffenden. So while Dunn is 'against most revolutions / all conformities' he is also, because of his origins on the geographical, cultural and political periphery, one of 'the inhabitants of opposition'. Coming from a place with a proudly separate political culture means one can 'never escape' its 'stale dreams / Old possibilities'. The end of the poem yearns for 'The existential clarity / Of love and nothing, the peace / Poets in patched trousers deserve' and roots it in adolescence i.e. before the dawning of an individual's mature political consciousness. However, the overdone whimsicality of the last line expresses an awareness of the unreality of such a 'peace'.

'Renfrewshire Traveller' implies that political poetry – poetry that is not dishonest and evasive – cannot be written before Dunn can answer questions about what Scotland is and what it means to be Scottish. The poem's repeated and insistent questions – 'Have I come back?', 'What have I come to?' – register a state of abjection. Scotland and Scottishness are not only synonymous with cultural stereotypes – 'I am Scots, a tartan tin box / Of shortbread' – but also with no work, an 'ache' and a 'brilliant lack'. Bernard O'Donoghue argues that in the poem 'we reach a voice that is the poet's own – or at least a characterization of the poet's own' (*RDD*, 43). The poem's voice convinces us because, like the central passage in 'Winter Orchard', the poet and the reader's interest in what is being said and how it is being said are synonymous. In contrast, too many poems in *The Happier Life* kept these things separate. In the context of Dunn's developing political poetry, the Scottish critic Cairns Craig reads 'Renfrewshire Traveller' against the background of an important period in Scottish left-wing thought. In the 1970s and 1980s, many Scottish intellectuals and politicians began to explore New Left ideas as a 'medium by which they could assert their commitment to working-class politics, while at the same time distancing those politics from the regional (and parochial) commitments of Scottishness'.[7] New Left politics was a way of placing Scotland on an international stage. The poem's questions suggest a similar re-positioning.

'Clydesiders' – one of Dunn's best known poems with its famous assertion 'My poems should be Clyde-built, crude and sure' – reconnects with a Scotland that is neither tartan nor shortbread and whose values are transferable beyond the regional. The poem begins in a Gents toilet: 'Men in boilersuits zip twice, Clyde-built'. Scotland is a place of labouring men and, the poem seems to hint with 'zip twice', of barely containable masculine power. The poem's later equation of poetry with manual labour converges with similar insistences in Seamus Heaney's 'Digging' and Tony Harrison's 'Lines to my Grandfathers'.[8] This belongs to a particular moment in post-war British poetry when working-class poets were embarking on a self-conscious colonization of the poetry establishment. It also expresses what Geoff Ward has identified as a wider twentieth-century anxiety about whether poetry is proper work for men.[9] However, this is less prominent than the Scotland the poem evokes. The Clyde conjures images of a nascent and unfulfilled internationalism in Scottish politics and makes a connection back to what Craig terms 'the excitements of potential revolution among the Clydesiders of the 1920s'.[10] The ending of the poem makes clear the kind of Scottishness that is to be operative:

> I made these marks, have gone back to London,
> No victim of my place, but mad for it.
> A shower of rain, my footprints melt and run.
> They'll follow to my life. I know they must.

The fact that Dunn's poems 'should be Clyde-built' suggests that they aren't yet. 'Should' voices an aspiration but also seems to suggest the unlikelihood of fulfilment. Poetry, it seems to be saying, 'should' be of some political use but it's difficult to imagine what such a poetry might look like especially when Dunn's most successful political poems are generally far from 'crude'. Indeed, as we shall see in the later work, Dunn is often at his most crude when he allows his loyalty to the diversity of inspiration to get the better of him. The footprints that 'follow' the poet portray an autobiographical imperative that is also an historical one. The importance of this imperative is underlined by the fact that it is expressed in Dunn's characteristic closing cadence. The 'usefulness' of the poem is perhaps located in the fact Dunn acknowledges the imperative and in doing so reserves the right to be 'crude' when necessary.

In the context of the history 'Clydesiders' evokes, there is an inevitability about *Love or Nothing* offering examples of autobiography as Scottish, political poetry. In poems like 'White Fields', 'The Competition' and 'Boys With Coats' we find further convincing examples of what O'Donoghue terms the 'characterization' of the poet's own voice (*LN*, 32–3, 43, 35). 'White Fields' looks back to 1948 and a childhood winter nightmare that the war wasn't yet over. The poem's second half rejects the complacent ease with which a sentence like 'No harm will come to us' can be uttered and accepted. This rejection is developed in one of Dunn's most evocative combinations of imagistic and discursive modes:

> White fields, your angled frost filed sharply
> Bright over undisturbed grasses, do not soothe
> As similes of innocence or idle deaths
> That must happen anyway, an unmoral blankness;
> . . . .

The imperative form of 'do' is crucial here. If the self is to be located in history through autobiographical poetry then that poetry must reject its own blandishments and seductions, its tendencies to glib symbol making and sermonizing. In contrast, 'The Competition' and 'Boys With Coats' are companion pieces, complementary reminiscences of early skirmishes in class war. Both poems feature the ten-year-old Dunn on a bus with a model Hurricane aeroplane. In 'The Competition' the young Dunn imagines kinship with a boy from a better school because they have the same model Hurricane but 'he called me a poor boy, who should shut up'. The result, the adult poet tells us, is that 'He'd never have a grudge as lovely as mine'. The concept of the grudge is an important one in Dunn's search for a political poetry. It is attached to the eponymous hero of 'Green Breeks' from Dunn's 1981 collection *St. Kilda's Parliament*; and it is the title of an important editorial Dunn published in *Stand* the year after *Love or Nothing*. I shall discuss it in detail in the next chapter. In 'Boys With Coats' the ten-year-old Dunn is in a superior position to 'a boy with no coat in the sleet and rain' to whom he gives 'my pocket-money and my model aeroplane'. Both poems end uncomfortably. 'The Competition' ends with Dunn beaten in a running race 'by someone from the Shotts Miners' Welfare Harriers Club' although he's 'convinced my best competitor was' the boy who'd told him to shut up. 'Boys with Coats' ends with a reminder that the Second World War 'in [...] serving justice served injustice' and with the young Dunn feeling 'radical that my lost Hurricane / Solved nothing in the sleet and rain'.

Love or Nothing comes to a close with a group of poems that attempt a different mode of politicizing: 'The Opportunity', 'The Dilemma', 'Restraint', 'The Malediction', 'The Estuarial Republic' and 'The Disguise' (*LN*, 50, 51, 58, 60, 61, 63). All abandon the expansive story telling of the autobiographical pieces in favour of stripped down forms and uncertain tones that partake uneasily of those already employed in 'Winter Orchard', 'Realisms' and 'Renfrewshire Traveller'. Sean O'Brien has noted that some of these poems 'demonstrate the difficulty of naming what was always there' (*RDD*, 72) and many proceed by indirection and even misdirection. For example, lines like 'Where nothing could be said against us' and 'It is perfection, to be without hope' come at the end of 'The Opportunity' and 'The Dilemma', poems that seem unable to bear the full weight of what the lines imply. Similarly, 'The Malediction' and 'The Estuarial Republic' promise much more than they actually deliver. The former is about a wish for snow although it may be possible that Dunn had in mind John Buchan's reference to 'the maledictions of great poets, whose hate confers an unwelcome immortality'. The latter seems to imply an alternative Scottish polis but turns out to be a fantasy about a savage country. This may, of course, look forward to Dunn's next volume *Barbarians*. These poems attempt to move beyond autobiography and the self-loathing and stereotypes of 'Renfrewshire Traveller'. If they read as failed experiments then that may be because as 'Restraint' concludes of its subject 'A long course in freedom / Hurts it. It cries out / And makes you tell lies.' *Love or Nothing*'s final poem 'The Disguise' is an *ars poetica* of a different type to 'Clydesiders':

> But I am smiling, and against you.
> There is an invective of grins, winks and fingers,
> . . . .
> Hidden by glum masks, the finest insult.

This statement of poetry as guerrilla activity also looks forward to *Barbarians* as does the poem's evocation of 'an absolute prosody [...] with the strength of an intricate machine' as an instrument of such activity. A poetry of smuggled invective also converges with Tony Harrison's project to use establishment forms as vehicles for experiences the establishment excludes.

Love or Nothing is, then, a decisive volume in terms of Dunn's developing sense of poetic and political responsibility. The penultimate poem of *Terry Street* was 'A Poem in Praise of the British' which could be read back into the book as a species of critical weather forecast. 'The Disguise's' observation that 'History is illiterate [...] Most live in the aftermath of its injustices' suggests not only a more fraught and vulnerable condition but also that someone will have to speak for and to history. However, *Love or Nothing* is important in other ways. We have already noted how the volume's first poem signalled a move into fiction and a willingness to follow the dictates of the imagination as often as those of politics. This is further evidenced in the playfulness of 'The Concert', the surrealism of 'Caledonian Moonlight' and 'Going to Bed' and the long homage to and short imitation of Larforgue in, respectively, 'The White Poet' and "Variations on the Words 'Solo' and 'Exhaust"' (*LN*, 48, 38, 39–40, 52–5, 57). In this context we might also note that a number of poems refer to the moon. It is these slightly uncanny moments and others like the mysterious and mystical white bird at the end of 'Winter Orchard' that would bear rich fruit later. As Bernard O'Donoghue has noted, if Dunn had only explored 'social responsibility and poetic form, *Elegies* would not have been able to reach [its] metaphysical heights' (*RDD*, 46).

3

Gestures of Affront

Barbarians is an important volume in Dunn's œuvre because it discovers, in Sean O'Brien's words, 'where a political poetry [is] to come *from*' (*RDD*, 72). The discovery is both ideological – it is impossible to discuss class without discussing nation – and poetic: we find Dunn almost totally abandoning free verse. It is worth quoting at length Dunn's comments – in his introduction for P. R. King and a *Poetry Wales* symposium on rhyme coeval with the book's publication – on the book's metrical organization:

> *Barbarians* is 'about' psychologies of class, racial and national superiorities – distempering, recalcitrant subjects. It is largely written in metre for the reason that someone in the persona of a barbarian would be expected to write them in grunts. A reversal of the standard myth of barbarism is obviously implicated in this stylistic ploy. The style of the book hopes to portray a gesture of affront to readers who might be expected to approve of a metrical way of writing, while finding the meaning of *Barbarians* disagreeable. (King, 225)

*

> My most recent use of rhyme and metre has been part of a strategy which is aware of the literary and political associations of verse. That is, while poems like 'Here be Dragons', 'In the Grounds', and 'The Student' flatter the stylistic preferences of orthodoxy, their content is at the same time ostensibly engaged in censuring that culture.[1]

Dunn's 'gesture of affront' and 'the literary and political associations of verse' are partly clarified by some of Wordsworth's remarks on metre in the Preface to the *Lyrical Ballads*. Wordsworth argues

> that by the act of writing in verse an Author makes a formal engagement that he will gratify certain known habits of association, that he not only thus apprizes the Reader that certain classes of ideas

and expressions will be found in his book, but that others will be carefully excluded.[2]

Dunn intends his 'stylistic ploy' to discomfort the reader because 'formal engagement' will be only superficially present and the 'ideas and expressions' in *Barbarians* will be those that are normally excluded. This, in turn, will cause the reader to reflect on the mechanisms and processes of exclusion. Dunn intends pleasure to be tempered with political awareness. However, one feels bound to point out that this is of necessarily limited effect. The usual reader of contemporary poetry is likely to be a liberal who will applaud Dunn's project. The key word in Dunn's comments on metre is, then, 'strategy'. His 'gesture of affront' is a way of signalling that he is writing out of a particular structure of feeling about poetry specifically and culture generally.

Rhyme and metre are not only strategic: they free the tentative intersubjectivity of Dunn's earlier work into full-blown monodrama. This relieves him of the difficulties of responsibly positioning himself and his subjects in free verse. The formal becomes the natural medium of the dramatic. Rhyme and metre also work to make recurring words and images more memorable and – combined with the book's three part structure of 'Barbarian Pastorals', poems about Scotland and general political poems – highlight a number of patterns. There is, for example, a complex structure made up of images of gates, entrances, waitings and exclusions. There are others concerning meanings of the word justice, 'the grudge' first encountered in 'The Competition' and the relationship between the connivances of official culture and the slyness required to negotiate them. These structures are laid over metrical structures which, in themselves, evoke ideas of civility and decency. The result is a powerful argument that civility and decency are founded on the misrecognition and victimization of the Other.

A complex interplay of class, nation and race is announced by the epigraphs to the book from Paul Nizan and to its first poem – 'The Come-on' – from Albert Camus. The two epigraphs are as follows:

> He was bored, but nevertheless he slowly grew further and further away from the hardship and simplicity of the workers, from his childhood environment. He somehow learned how to behave, as

they say. Without realizing it, he cut himself off from his own people.... He thought he was merely bored, but secretly he was flattered at being included. Some forces drew him towards the bourgeoisie; other forces sought to retard his transition.

The truth of life was on the side of the men who returned to their poor houses, on the side of the men who had not 'made good'.

*

...the guardian, the king's son who kept watch over the gates of the garden in which I wanted to live.

(B, 10)

The Nizan epigraph emphasizes how entry into culture involves a process of assimilation that leads to the alienation of the working-class individual from himself and his origins. The Camus epigraph stresses culture as a matter of privileges not rights. Similarly, as David Kinloch observes, 'The principal thrust of Nizan's published work was to show how every aspect of culture was penetrated by a bourgeois, humanist ethos. "La culture est bourgeois ou elle n'est pas", he wrote' (RDD, 159). It is this that is dramatized in 'The Come-on'. The poem, characterized in line three as 'the bitter ooze from my grudge', airs the grievance of a man and a poet and, indeed, a class who find that the compromises marginalized individuals are expected to make with the centre are not returned. 'The bitter ooze' might be characterized as the question: how can the place of 'enchanting, beloved texts' also be the site of enduring class prejudice? Part of Dunn's answer is to turn the language of the centre against itself by placing scare quotes around 'background', 'coals in the bath', 'professional classes', 'rights', 'standards', 'authority', 'poetry' and 'disinterested tradition'. These terms belong to an accepted discourse about culture and society and to highlight them in this way not only reveals them as a privileged discourse but emphasizes their alienating effects. Recognizable words and phrases are made curious with the result that the standard starts to look like the non-standard. The language of the centre starts to look illusory and delusional.

Contemporary reviewers insisted on misreading 'The Come-on' and the other 'Barbarian Pastorals' as predominantly personal. Anne Stevenson saw the poems as 'warnings to himself and his friends rising on the social ladder' and Peter Porter commended Dunn's 'brilliant polemical expression [of] his resentment of metropolitan smoothies who dismiss all worlds but their own.'[3] Porter is nearer the mark but it is worth noting that 'The Come-on' is set within the institution of education. In the early 1970s, the educational policies that had benefited Dunn's generation were under increasing attack from the Right. Between 1969 and 1975, a series of *Black Papers On Education*, edited by C.B. Cox and A.E. Dyson, attacked comprehensive education and argued that 'progressive education [is] breaking down faith in high culture'. One of Margaret Thatcher's actions as Education Minister under Edward Heath was to withdraw legislation imposing comprehensivation on local authorities. The *Black Papers* were symptomatic of a wider reaction against the alleged excesses of the 1960s and a corresponding desire for greater control.[4] The desire partly prompted James Callaghan's famous speech on education given at Ruskin College, Oxford, in October 1976. He referred to the *Black Papers* and commented that 'those who claim to defend standards [...] in reality are simply seeking to defend old privileges and inequalities.'[5] Although 'The Come-on' was first published in 1974, it clearly responds to the same shift: 'Listen now to the 'professional classes' / Renewing claims to 'rights' // [...] Decency of 'standards' (*B*, 13). At the same time, beyond the confines of educational debate, there was increasing pessimism on the Left as it became clear that cultural institutions were not only unchanged but remained as powerful as ever. In this context, it is notable that 'In The Grounds', 'Here Be Dragons', 'The Student' and 'An Artist Waiting...' show the centre undisturbed by 'our rabble-dreams' (*B*, 15, 16, 19, 21). Finally, 'Barbarian Pastorals' may also have a specifically poetic derivation. Writing in 1980, Peter Jones and Michael Schmidt drew attention to 'The ascendancy of the academy over poets and poetry in the 1970s' manifested in an increased demand for teachable poetry.[6]

Walls breached with the formalities of the tradition they enclose relate to the idea of 'the grudge' that appears at the beginning of the poem as well as in earlier poems such as 'The Competition' (*LN*, 34). The complex meaning of the term for Dunn is revealed by an editorial with the same title he wrote for *Stand* magazine in the mid-1970s.[7] The piece explores how the working-class writer is to make cultural products that are genuinely oppositional in genres that are fundamentally bourgeois: 'His work is [...] directed at an audience who do not receive it; instead, it is received by an audience of those he is against.' (4) The struggle of the working-class writer is located around 'the effort to secure a connection between poetics and the politics of his class.' (5) The connection is to be found in 'commitment' which Dunn calls 'the idea under which a working class poet can organize the sundry circumstances which belong to him and which cohere in the form of beliefs about the world.' This, in turn, leads to a counter-narrative of 'poetry as the vision of its own classless society and not [...] the instrument of class ascendancy.' Throughout the struggle, each writer will have his or her own version of the grudge.[8] In Dunn's case it is the memory of being told not to sit on a particular wall as a child: 'Poetry is like that wall. There are people who think they own poetry. They think poetry 'serves' *them*. It doesn't; and when it does it is being exclusive and partial. So I have a grudge'(6).

All this clarifies how 'a metrical way of writing [...] hopes to portray a gesture of affront' to a particular constituency of readers who will also be deafened 'With the dull staccato of our typewriters.' In fact, I do not think it is stretching a point to see these typewriters in metrical terms because it seems that Dunn – a little paradoxically – wants metre to do two kinds of work simultaneously. It will be a 'sly' and 'cunning' means of entering the 'culture of connivance'. At the same time, it will be so 'deafening' it will upset that 'connivance' by perhaps doing the opposite of what Anthony Easthope in *Poetry As Discourse* ascribes to 'the counterpoint of the pentameter': 'Recognition of the work of metric *production* – and so of the poem as constructed artifice – is suppressed in favour of a notion of the poem as spontaneously generated *product*.'[9] [Original emphasis]. In this context, the equation of metre with 'the dull staccato of [...] typewriters' is a way of equating cultural production generally and the writing of poetry specifically with real work, an equation that also occurs in the work of Seamus Heaney and Tony Harrison.[10] It also figures the effort of those who do not feel that culture and its production are part of their natural inheritance. Wordsworth's 'Preface' also illuminates how metre is part of 'cunning'. He argues that, there can be little doubt but that more pathetic situations and sentiments, that is, those which have a greater proportion of pain connected with them, may be endured in metrical composition, especially in rhyme, than in prose. (264)

If we put this together with Dunn's remarks about his use of metre and rhyme in *Barbarians*, then endurance and what Dunn calls 'disagreeable' meaning come to have different implications for the usual reader of poetry and the working-class writer. Metre and rhyme become a way of getting 'disagreeable' material past the reader's expectations but they might also be a way of enabling the working-class writer to deal with such material. Metre and rhyme temper the writer's own pain in dealing with his 'grudge'. In terms of 'The Come-on', they are a means of putting up with it and of being able to carry on with the struggle.

The rest of the 'Barbarian Pastorals' places both suppression and resultant grudge in a wider context. 'In the Grounds' (*B*, 15–16) examines how the popular pastime of visiting country houses re-inserts us into an oppressive class narrative while 'Here be Dragons' (*B*, 16–17) looks at how Roman writings about barbaric and semi-mythical races abroad 'flattered Rome, to keep its regnum sure.' 'Gardeners' (*B*, 17-18) and 'The Student' (*B*, 19-20) are carefully placed and dated – respectively, 'England, Loamshire, 1789' and 'Renfrewshire, 1820' – in order to highlight the 'affront' of placing revolutionary and republican narratives in classical forms. 'An Artist Waiting in a Country House' (*B*, 21–4), if not a 'barbarian pastoral' *per se*, serves to highlight both the condescending relationship between bourgeois patron and artist and how such a relationship implicates the artist – like the weekend visitor to a stately home – in 'An architecture of success and wealth / In far, disreputable trades, or in / The purse of government.' (*B*, 21) In the words of 'The Student' lamenting the suppression of Scottish republicanism

> Beneath our banners I was marching for
> My scholarship of barley, secret work
> On which authority must slam its door
> As Rome on Goth, Byzantium on Turk.

(*B*, 20)

This image of centres of civilization as the sites of a kind of barbarism through exclusion is echoed throughout *Barbarians*. In 'Empires' (*B*, 26) the aftermath of 'All the dead Imperia' is to have left the millions they both 'ruled' and 'fooled [...] destitute.' Similarly, in 'Ballad of the Two Left Hands' (*B*, 41-3) the 'obsolete' shipyard workers of the Clyde dream of an ideal opposite of centres like Rome, Byzantium and, presumably, London: 'In an illegal bar / They toast the city still to come / Where truth and justice meet' (*B*, 43). It is in lines like these that a particular image of Scotland – implicit in Dunn's earlier volumes – begins to emerge. For while Part II of *Barbarians* might at first seem only to investigate the destitution that results from a lack of truth and justice in specifically Scottish terms, it also mounts a counter-argument that destitution is not the end of the matter. For example, the Clydesiders who toast the future clearly do not share the political quietism and passivity of the inhabitants of the silent urban England of *Terry Street*, *The Happier Life* or *Love or Nothing*. Scotland may ostensibly, in the terms of 'The Disguise', seem to live out the aftermath of history's injustices but there is an equally strong sense in which its 'loneliness of virtue' (*THL*, 53) is as transhistorical as the colonialism which disadvantaged it. Here Dunn's project to give a voice to his class starts to become inseparable from giving a voice to his nation. The story of 'The Musician' – the carpenter playing the jigs of '[his] local tradition' but wanting to 'break through / To the public of Bach and Beethoven' (*B*, 37) – takes on a wider resonance. It is interestingly glossed by a comment in the interview given to William Oxley in which Dunn attempts to distinguish Scottish ideas of class, culture and nation:

> This could be a Scottish trait – the Scottish arts are direct, libertarian and unconcerned with aristocratic values. It's one of the factors that makes Scottish civilisation unique. Hence, too, what I believe to be the Scottish tragedy – that the democratic spirit of Scotland, or, more accurately, its potential has never had the opportunity to express the people who created it, but has always been in opposition. (Oxley, 17)

What the two passages suggest, I think, is that Dunn's work brings class and nation into relation because his conceptions of both manifest a convergence of internal contradictions. One feels bound to ask why the fiddler, secure in his 'local tradition', should have any interest in reaching a classical audience. Similarly, if there is a 'unique' Scottish civilisation then it is difficult to understand why its people would pay any attention to English civilisation let alone expend energy opposing it. The second question is perhaps more readily answered than the first. Scottish historian T. C. Smout contends that Scottishness is a 'duality of consciousness [being Scottish and British] [...] a contradiction within the citizen that is never resolved.'[11] The periphery and the lower classes internalize the centre's view of them. Dunn's generation was brought up in a period before the 'margins v. centre' opposition that defines large areas of contemporary cultural analysis had any currency. This helps to explain the frustrated ambition Dunn ascribes to the fiddler for it seems more likely that Dunn is dramatizing his own *specifically literary* anxieties. Dunn's poem is haunted by anxieties about what value a local tradition really has.

Part II of *Barbarians* also contains a group of broadly elegiac poems. 'Elegy for the lost Parish', 'Watches of Grandfathers', 'Portrait Photograph, 1915', 'Alice' and 'Drowning' are characterized by words like 'requiem', 'consolation', 'funerals' and 'posterity' (*B*, 33, 34, 35, 35, 37). The group focuses on what 'Portrait Photograph, 1915' calls 'a sense of posterity in the eyes of descendants' and in doing so asserts the value of individual histories and private lives. Indeed, the lives portrayed in these poems might be precisely those which, in the words of 'The Come-on', 'might just as well / Not exist when the vile / Come on with their 'coals in the bath' stories'. The short poem 'Glasgow Schoolboys, Running Backwards' says that the struggle against such stories never ends:

> High wind ... They turn their backs to it, and push.
> Their crazy strides are chopped in little steps.
> And all their lives, like that, they'll have to rush
> Forwards in reverse, always holding their caps.
>
> (*B*, 39)

In the interview given to John Haffenden in November 1979, Dunn makes a telling comparison between himself and a Scottish poet he admires George Mackay Brown:

> In my mind, the better community is in the future; in Mackay's mind, it's in the past. My enterprise I suppose is to recuperate

tolerance and benevolence, to preserve it into the time when technology produces the sort of cosmopolis that we're all going to live with inevitably [...] [Mackay Brown] can depict history without that portrayal conveying the germs of its own revolution and reformation.... (Haffenden, 29)

Key poems in Dunn's 1981 collection *St. Kilda's Parliament* had already been written and published in magazines. 'John Wilson in Greenock, 1786', 'Tannahill' and 'Green Breeks' are all concerned with history as a project of recuperation, revolution and reformation (*SKP*, 47–9, 52–6, 57–61). 'Green Breeks' seeks to counter what it terms 'mendacious annals' and passages from Dunn's later writings highlight the urgency of his triple project. His concluding remarks in his Introduction to *The Faber Book of Twentieth-Century Scottish Poetry* (1992) portray cultural activity at the periphery as synonymous with demands for self-determination: 'It has been a hectic century for Scottish poetry, one filled with thrilling turbulence, and in which the stakes have been high – the survival of a national identity' (xlvi). In Dunn's description of his Tayport home in 'Here and There' in his 1988 collection *Northlight* as 'a regenerate / Country in which to reconstruct a self / From local water, timber, light and earth' the sense of that self is as much national as individual (*N*, 26). The reconstructed self is certainly involved in disgruntled opposition to the fact that 'the mighty X installed / The government a quarter voted for' but, more importantly, it is implicated in the framing and answering of much more complex questions. One of these is certainly 'What's absolute in nations?' which, as lines later in the poem make clear, is also a yearning for a transhistorical answer:

> History makes the answers difficult:
> It's yesterday; tomorrow's not tomorrow.
> So carry your kicked arse in a wheelbarrow.
> You're colonized! Maybe you didn't know![12]

As 'It's yesterday' underlines, he wants to resist the strong tendencies in the Scottish cultural self towards sentimentality, anachronism and what his Faber Introduction calls the 'archaizing mode' (xlvi). However, history makes the answers difficult for another reason: each Scottish writer is to some extent condemned to encounter and contest the predicament which Edwin Muir identified in Walter Scott and which Dunn quotes in his Faber Introduction:

> [...] [Scott] spent most of his days in a hiatus, in a country, that is to say, which was neither a nation nor a province, and had, instead of a centre, a blank, an Edinburgh, in the middle of it. But this Nothing in which Scott wrote was not merely a spatial one; it was a temporal Nothing as well [...] Scott, in other words, lived in a community which was not a community, and set himself to carry on a tradition which was not a tradition; and the result was that his work was an exact reflection of his predicament. His picture of life had no centre, because the environment in which he lived had no centre. (xxxii)

This seems to accept that questions of Scottish nationhood are doomed to be elusive. However, another important question that suggests that this is not the case would be asked in *Dante's Drum-kit*: 'What has a decent poetry left to teach?' (37) Dunn's interview with Robert Crawford underlines decency as a key concept in his poetry as both subject and perspective. Decency is one way of describing the 'ethic' of 'remote communities [...] which when contrasted with the priorities of more up to date sophisticated contemporary societies and communities looks increasingly valuable' (Crawford, 26). Most importantly, it is a way of looking:

> Decency is in *knowing* about what's happened, and what can happen, and of being aware of the possible squalor and toxicity of life, but at the same time – without evasions – of refusing to allow one's own life to become disablingly contaminated with the crimes against humanity and nature which in our century are so *visible*. (Crawford, 30 – original emphasis)

The poetics developed in *Terry Street* and after has a particular enabling power when applied to Scottish subjects. As W. N. Herbert valuably points out, poems on Scottish subjects from *St. Kilda's Parliament* onwards make spaces where 'myth and fact can approach each other and [...] establish a dialogue'. The result is that 'the stifled voice of the subjected past' is recomposed into 'a series of hymns to possibility' (*RDD*, 131). Dunn, in fact, can be said to be producing his own particular version of what postcolonial critics term resistance literature. Dunn resists by a series of reimaginative cultural and political returns to important moments and sites. The title poem of *St.*

Kilda's Parliament, with its careful dates, 1879–1979, and subtitle 'The photographer revisits his picture' is emblematic of such returns. On one level, the poem has a clear political meaning. Its idealization of 'a remote democracy', a parliament literally lost through depopulation, combines with '1979' – the date of the Devolution Referendum when Scots voted for but were denied an independent Scottish parliament – to record the most recent instance of the democratic spirit of Scotland being unable to express the people who created it. St. Kilda's identity, until its depopulation, as Scotland's most remote community becomes a metonym of political hopelessness and marginalization. However, the poem should not be taken as narrowly programmatic. Verbs of looking dominate as much as they did in *Terry Street* and continue Dunn's explorations of what is involved in observation and the complex interrelations of subject and object.

The Scottish context of the poem places these explorations in the context of 'internal colonialism' i.e. the idea that master-slave relationships can exist between areas within one country that parallel those between colonies and a colonial power. The poem begins in a register that mimics the type of old-fashioned anthropological investigations which portrayed a quaint, romanticized primitivism. Here is a way of life that is simple to the point of harshness but also somehow picturesque. The men are 'barefooted', displaying pride in their 'small life' but ignorant, the photographer tells us, 'of what a pig, a bee, a rat, / Or a rabbit look like' (*SKP*, 13). The passage towards the end of the poem in which the photographer tells us he took his picture in the same year he was recording the 'distressed cities', 'lost empires' and 'writhing flesh' of 'that larger franchise' makes clear that this is a familiar narrative of a decadent and impoverished centre appropriating the apparent cultural 'purity' of the primitive Other. This narrative is disturbed, as the looking of *Terry Street* was disturbed, by the returning gaze of the Other. The men outside their parliament ultimately 'escape' the photograph: the photographer cannot tell if they are 'Benevolent, or malign', 'Wise men or simpletons' and it is here that the subtitle of the poem begins to make sense. The photographer cannot really revisit his picture but the imaginary scene allows Dunn and the poem to stand outside time:

> Here I whittle time, like a dry stick,
> From sunrise to sunset, among the groans
> And sighings of a tongue I cannot speak,
> Outside a parliament, looking at them,
> As they, too, must always look at me
> Looking through my apparatus at them
> Looking.
>
> (*SKP*, 15)

The moment of the photograph is all such encounters, continuing to happen, perpetually recreating a dialectic of appropriation and resistance. The moment is timeless in another way too for it allows Dunn to stand outside the seductive 'archaizing mode' of discussions about Scotland. The important thing about St. Kilda is not its eventual depopulation but the spirit of its people and their relationship to place. 'St. Kilda's Parliament' is a lesson in how to view oneself and one's place of origin in ways that do not replicate the perspectives of the centre.

Dunn's intersubjectivity becomes refined into a way of describing Scotland but the question of *what* can be described remains vexed. 'The Apple-Tree' offers 'my missionary fruits' as correctives to stereotypical views of 'our coarse consent / To drunken decency and sober violence / Our paradox of ways' and a complacency that sees 'quick links forced from character to climate' (*SKP*, 16). 'An Address on the Destitution of Scotland' is set in 'this undeclared Republic' which is described as a barbarian encampment. The poem's determination to see Scotland's condition clearly is evident in phrases such as 'destitute polity', 'nocturne of modernity', 'outcast silence' and 'dens of extinction'. Nonetheless, the poem seems unable to avoid its own 'paradox of ways'. The last line – 'Sing me your songs in the speech of timber and horse' – seems redolent of the 'archaizing mode' Dunn would later identify in Scottish poetry (*SKP*, 19, 20). Similarly, Robert Crawford reads the line as 'summoning a country which can be present only as elegy' (*RDD*, 114). At the same time, the poem's concern with return suggests the line may be read as a return to origins, an attempt to make a new start that will not lead to untransacted 'Red desires'. Dunn's estimate of George Mackay Brown underlines another paradox inherent in such a return: how to make a present and future Scotland that is modern but not part of the technological 'cosmopolis'. As Dunn observed in a 1990 essay on Norman MacCaig, 'Scotland is not an easy subject with which to relax, especially when you take into account that the Scotland envisaged by literature over the past 250 years is not the Scotland of political reality.'[13]

Subsequent poems explore where a Scotland that makes vision into reality is to come from so that its 'democratic spirit [...] its potential' can have 'the opportunity to express the people who created it' (Oxley, 17). 'Witch-girl', Dunn's own blurb tells us, recounts the tale of 'a witch who was not a witch but the forgotten *anima* of Scotland' (*SKP*, 22–3). As Robert Crawford points out, the poem's last line where the poet '[hears] her breathing in the wood and stone' makes this *anima* 'at once historical and transhistorical' (*RDD*, 114). In doing so it echoes both the end of 'An Address...' and the earlier poem 'Fixed' which describes Clydeside as 'In all its clay and wooden parts, / A perfect place' (*THL*, 66). Scotland's democratic spirit is literally earthed and Dunn's project would seem to be to repair its broken circuitry. 'Washing the Coins' (*SKP*, 24–5) describes childhood potato picking and is 'autobiographical and it happened the way the poem says' (Oxley, 17). The poem's detailed description of hard physical work not only corrects any residual romanticism in a vision of a nation of 'timber and horse' and 'wood and stone' but also portrays Scotland as a victim of internal colonialism. The work gives the young Dunn 'something in common with bedraggled Irish' co-workers and later in the poem the farmer's wife 'couldn't tell my face / From an Irish's boy's'. The bleak conclusion is 'It is not good to feel you have no future' which suggests that while there may be values in the past much of it must be rejected. 'Galloway Motor Farm' is another elegy for Scotland's destitution which can't quite resolve the paradoxes. The speaker says he will have been glad to have lived 'Within this stung bubble where antiquities / Freshen, where they breathe the present tense' but the next stanza ends with lamentation: 'Scotland, come back / From the lost ground of your dismantled lands'. (*SKP*, 27).

'The Harp of Renfrewshire' is one of Dunn's finest poems and is full of subtle and surprising turns of phrase – 'soft disputes', 'ground's secret lexicon' – but its portrayal of a map as a living, audible record highlights the difficulties involved in re-rooting a future Scotland in ancient origins (*SKP*, 30). The poem's movement from 'Annals of the trilled R, gently stroked L' to 'A granary of whispers rinsed in dew' make it as elegiac as the Scottish poems which precede it. 'Whispers' continues those poems' portrayal of a country that is either silent or barely audible. The last line underlines the elegiac note with its echo of 'Winter Graveyard' where 'inscriptions [...] Rinse their loving vocabularies / In the light of dreams'. The effect of 'The Harp of Renfrewshire' is, as Sean O'Brien notes, to imagine Scotland with 'a simultaneous yes, no and perhaps' (*RDD*, 76).

In the interview with John Haffenden, Dunn notes that 'Tannahill' and 'John Wilson in Greenock, 1786' 'should be in the first sequence of *Barbarians*' and goes on to say that they are part of a projected Scottish *poètes maudits* (Haffenden, 25). One assumes that 'Green Breeks', which retells an episode from the life of Sir Walter Scott, is also part of the project. Dunn goes on to describe his putative project to John Haffenden as 'almost like a critical work' (Haffenden, 27) but the poems are much more than a species of literary archaeology. In the context of post-1979 Devolution Referendum Scotland, they reveal the workings of official culture and politics. The project of 'Tannahill', 'John Wilson in Greenock, 1786' and 'Green Breeks' is to free their subjects retrospectively from appropriation and thereby reassert connections between individual voice and national identity.

Robert Tannahill, Dunn tells Haffenden, was a Paisley weaver who 'wrote songs and began to pick up the threads, so to speak, of Burns's work' but who later 'drowned himself with his poems' after rejection by an Edinburgh publisher (Haffenden, 25–6). 'The threads of Burns's work' refer to the political radicalism and genuinely proletarian voice of his early poetry that was sentimentalized by the Edinburgh literary scene – 'Their ploughman poet' – and then suppressed by his employment as an excise-man. The fact that Tannahill refused such a compromise contributed to his tragic end but also made him a different poet:

> A wabster's craft would teach a man
> To live with art as an artisan.
> As you could weave, teach me to scan
>   And turn a rhyme

> Fraternally, like Caliban
> His low sublime.
>
> *(SKP,* 54)

Tannahill allows Dunn to equate poetry with manual labour. More importantly, the image of Caliban reappears in *Dante's Drum-kit* (117) where the poet's request to his 'Misshapen' form to 'Tell me the secrets of your lost / Reality, your Pictish origin' recalls Tannahill's 'Lost, watery verse'. Caliban stands in both passages as an image of oppression but also of something forever recalcitrant, resistant to appropriation. Caliban is the 'unnoble' savage, the unacceptable barbarian. 'Tannahill' is also clearly about finding the right form and this inevitably reads back into the earlier Scottish poems concerned with the future form of the nation. Similarly, as in 'The Harp of Renfrewshire' language is synonymous with nation: Tannahill, like Burns 'could hone / A merry R, lick till they shone / Gently stroked Ls' (*SKP,* 53).

The monodrama 'John Wilson in Greenock, 1786' recounts how another poet was forced to abandon writing poetry by his employers at Greenock Grammar School in order to keep his job. Burns is, again, a defining presence for 1786 was the date of the publication in Kilmarnock of the book on which his fame rests, *Poems, Chiefly in the Scottish Dialect.* John Wilson, speaking in 1786 and therefore unable to know that Burns would later be effectively silenced, sees him as the symbol of an uncompromised and uncompromising achievement. Like 'Tannahill', the poem is concerned with what can and can't be said about Scotland –

> I see a stream, but I must not discern
> A heathen Georgic in a Lowland burn.
>
> *(SKP,* 60)

– and uses similar language to the earlier Scottish poems in its 'sanctified / [...] water, wood and stone' and 'unwritten ghost'. Dunn allows himself the luxury of having Wilson address the future and assert that 'Those who come after me' will be able to 'claim that *to be free* / Is carried on the back of poetry.' 'Green Breeks' makes even more explicit connections between politics and what stanza five calls 'the quicklime of [...] ordered literature.' The poem retells an incident from the early life of

Sir Walter Scott, one of a series of mock battles between middle-class boys and 'the street-boys'. The 'Mendacious annals' of both Scott himself and his biographer Lockhart come to stand for the larger distortions of history. Dunn notes the fact that the young Scott and his friends 'were organized / Into a 'company' or 'regiment' by the same Duchess-Countess Sutherland 'who'd later 'clear' her kinsmen from her land'. He goes on to draw analogies between the way Scott and his friends used a sword to achieve decisive victory and then attempted to compensate for the injury with 'smart money'.

Although the injured 'street boy' refused the money and retained his pride and 'nursed his lovely grudge' he was unable to escape Scott's aestheticization of him into 'peasant baroque' and 'a Dying Gaul'. In contrast, says Dunn,

> I let him *be*.
> He is my light, conspirator and spy.
> He is perpetual. He is my country.
> He is my people's minds, when they perceive
> A native truth persisting in the weave
> Of shabby happenings. When they turn their cheeks
> The other way, he turns them back, Green Breeks.
>
> (*SKP*, 50)

'Green Breeks' reveals culture both as a means through which discourses of dominance and subservience are perpetuated and as the place where they must be contested. At the same time, the poem not only makes clear Scottish complicity in a class system but challenges what the social historian A. Allan MacLaren has termed the 'Scottish Myth' whose egalitarian fantasies have fostered beliefs that 'the social gap between the classes was never important.'[14]

'Tannahill', 'John Wilson in Greenock, 1786' and 'Green Breeks' together with 'St. Kilda's Parliament: 1879-1979' resist the characteristic operations of official culture. The way in which the poems seek to free their subjects from appropriation or suppression is also an attempt to stand outside history and to release a transhistorical voice and national identity which will resist the transhistorical nature of colonialism itself. In the context of Scotland, however, *St. Kilda's Parliament*, like the later *Northlight* and *Dante's Drum-kit*, gives a sense of language and voice located firmly in place and in actual earth. 'The Harp of

Renfrewshire' refers to a 'Land-language' and opposes the 'Mendacious annals' of 'Green Breeks' with 'Annals of the trilled R, gently stroked L'. These distinctive phonetic sounds appear throughout Dunn's more recent work. In 'Here and There' Dunn says that 'Without a Scottish voice [...] / I'm a contortionist [...] / swallowing [...] R's' and 'Audenesques for 1960' highlights the 'Scottish accent's / Rhotocistic R and slobbering lambdacism'.[15]

So what does it mean to say, as Dunn does in 'Witch-girl', for example, that some essential part of the Scottish national soul can be heard 'breathing in wood and stone'? (*SKP*, 23) In the context of the political consciousness of Dunn's poetry, its nursing of grudges and alertness to cultural formations and the constructedness of the subject, offering an argument that essential meaning is located in the non-human appears both inadequate and unrealistic. In a wider, late-twentieth century context of postmodernism and poststructuralism, an organicist view of language might seem as naïve and mystificatory in its own way as Scott's romanticizing of Green Breeks. Indeed, 'The Miniature Metro' uses the whiskey-conjured shade of Rimbaud to show an awareness of the self-congratulatory fictions involved in equating, like Seamus Heaney, pens with spades or poetry with manual labour (*SKP*, 77–8). In the context of O'Brien's 'simultaneous yes, no and perhaps' the poem takes some delight in registering the criticisms while telling us it's ignoring them. *St. Kilda's Parliament* clearly does have an archaeological project similar to Heaney's but with a very different end in mind. Heaney's diggings seek a comforting cultural derivation for present barbarities. Dunn's ploughings on his 'horse-writer' seek to overturn the concept of barbarism as a stifling fiction. Agricultural work and its language is one of many starting points for his wider project of resistance through reimagining. The evocation of a 'land-language' must be read as a defining component in Dunn's efforts to re-place the traditional opposition of England and Scotland. In place of the portrayal of an industrialized, progressive England and of a Scotland that has some unique institutions but is essentially picturesque and semi-rural, Dunn is able to rediscover a rooted form of life. It is another means of accessing the transhistorical, of recovering a source of identity and meaning that resides not in the non-human but in the fact that people have lived and worked and left their imprints on the non-human. The key phrase in 'The Harp of Renfrewshire' is 'A darg of conversations' where 'darg' is both day's work and primitive forge. Nation, too, it seems is to be located and forged in the imprint of the lives and talk of other people.

St. Kilda's Parliament not only shows Dunn grappling with questions of community and nation but also reveals the profoundly elegiac nature of his poetry. In 'The Miniature Metro' Dunn tells Rimbaud of 'my philosophy of departures / In which are regretted leave-takings of things' (*SKP*, 77) and the word 'lost' tolls throughout the book. 'Lamp-posts' manages to be an elegy of sorts while registering political horrors and even the minor 'Rose' imagines making up 'a ritual / for the departures of roses' (*SKP*, 76, 34). Dunn would comment to Bernard O'Donoghue about his next full-length collection *Elegies* that 'In style, the poems [...] differ little if at all from earlier writing. The stylistic habits acquired in previous books were all I had to hold on to as I worked' (O'Donoghue, 48).

4

Innermost Dialects

Dunn's next book was not a full-length collection but the sequence *Europa's Lover* published as a pamphlet by Bloodaxe Books in 1982. Europe and, more specifically, France had been a powerful presence in Dunn's poetry since 'The Musical Orchard' in his second volume *The Happier Life*. *Europa's Lover* is of a different order than Dunn's earlier homages to Jules Laforgue, Robert Desnos and ratatouille. Neil Corcoran has noted that its style is 'at once phantasmagorically gnomic and lucidly precise, and therefore [effects] the most secure bridge Dunn has yet erected between the almost separable kinds of poetry he has written'[1]. Dunn had told John Haffenden that

> Desnos often managed to write surrealist poems in rhyme and metre, which I find tremendously exciting, and I think the kind of poet I'd like to be – if I could just get rid of the subject matter I'm shackled with, simply as a fact of who I am – is the kind Desnos was. [...] Desnos is classically European, too, like my other heroes, Camus and Nizan.
>
> [Haffenden, 28–9]

In contrast, the modes of writing that have tended to be praised and rewarded in post-war mainstream British poetry – centralist naturalism on the one hand, a more or less politicized regionalism on the other – underline British poetry's isolation from the 'classically European'. *Europa's Lover* can be read as a manifesto of creative relocation as its epigraph from Paul Nizan makes clear: 'Men make more than one native land for themselves [...] for men are born more than once'. The sequence is full of characteristic Dunn phrases such as 'archives of sun and rain', 'a dusk-rinsed smoke' and 'lapsed literacies / Singing in earth and water' but these are written into a different history and set of cultural traditions. The result is that what Neil Corcoran would call the almost separable elements of his work – the lyric shading into the surreal, the historical reimaginings, the contemporary engagements – are given permission to co-exist by having a European derivation discovered for them. Europa tells the poet to 'lose that obsession / [...] which deals in / Survival, prosperity and salvation' (*SP*, 212). In its place he must discover Europe's 'dear munificent existences' and learn that 'we are dressed in history and shaped [...] in the races entwined like fingers' (*SP*, 217). Recurring images of weddings and wedding clothes are echo-homages to Desnos but also underline Europe as a place of entwining. To be dressed in history is also to be wedded to it. To be European is to recognize both the debts one owes to the dead and their legacies to us.

Paying debts to the dead and recognizing what they want for us are central to Dunn's next collection *Elegies*. Published in 1985 to great critical acclaim, it was the book that made Dunn famous, winning the Whitbread Poetry Award in 1986 and the Whitbread Book of the Year Award the following year. Its thirty-nine poems commemorate Dunn's first wife Lesley who died from cancer in 1981 and most of the poems were written in the year after her death. Dunn's accounts of the writing of the book in various interviews have described his initial reticence about whether to write the poems at all and, once they were written, whether to publish them. His accounts have also focused on the word 'natural'. Dunn told Robert Crawford that he had 'to ascertain to myself that this was a natural thing to do: something that a poet to whom this had happened should do' (31) and made a similar point to William Oxley (19). In the interview given to Bernard O'Donoghue, Dunn says that the writing of *Elegies* enabled him to come to 'some sort of understanding that poetry is natural and benevolent'. Naturalness is an important consideration in the writing of elegy, a genre that is perhaps more self-consciously and self-reflexively literary than any other. Canonical elegy is usually a matter of male poets commemorating other male poets as in Swinburne's 'Ave atque Vale' or Matthew Arnold's 'Thyrsis'. A high degree of stylistic and structural linguistic patterning and echoes of poetic antecedents also characterize elegy. When, for example, Matthew Arnold in 'Thyrsis' refers to 'a single elm-tree bright' he is alluding simultaneously to the 'fav'rite tree' in Thomas Gray's 'Elegy Written in a Country Churchyard' and to the elm tree in one of the earliest pastoral idylls, Theocritus's 'First Idyll' dating from the fourth century B.C.

The concern to avoid the refuge of excessive literariness – what one poem calls 'aesthetic pain' (*E*, 49) – is an important strand in the book. Even the plural of its title seems to contest the assumption that what Dunn has termed 'a love and its loss' (O'Donoghue, 47) could be contained in a single poem. The experience of reading *Elegies* is what might be termed 'elegy dispersed': the book contains, among other things, sonnets, *terza rima*, imitations of classical elegy, swathes of discursive and soliloquizing blank verse, urban and pastoral lyrics, and fantasy narratives. This makes *Elegies* exactly like Dunn's previous collections with, of course, the key difference that all the poems orbit the same subject. The need to write against the English canon and its self-reflexiveness is also clear in the book's epigraph from the nineteenth-century Italian poet Giosuè Carducci. Dunn uses four lines from 'Il Canto dell'Amore', the concluding poem to his book of political satires *Gambi ed Epodi* which, Paul Hamilton notes, are a 'command to love and so share a vision of Italy's sacred future' and an 'invocation of a communal hymn to peace' (*RDD*, 95). Dunn signals not consolation but transformation. As he told William Oxley, 'A life and its love had to be commemorated before a new life could begin' (Oxley, 19). The comment reproduces the classical elegiac movement to renewal and transformation. Milton's 'Lycidas' ends with its singer looking to 'Tomorrow to fresh woods, and pastures new'. Similarly, Shelley's 'Adonais' ends – less comfortably – with universal Light, Beauty and Benediction 'consuming' its author's own 'cold mortality' and translating him to where the soul of Keats 'like a Star / Beacons from the abode where the Eternals are'. The two examples underline, then, that renewal and transformation are elegy's destinations: Dunn uses Carducci to signal they are his starting points.

It is also worth noting two other significant departures Dunn makes from the genre. First, unlike 'Lycidas', say, or Tennyson's 'In Memoriam', *Elegies* is not overly concerned with the shock of its subject's death. Once Lesley's cancer had been diagnosed, her death became a possibility. Second, *Elegies* follows a trend in other English elegiac poetry of the last thirty years in being highly autobiographical. The poet places himself inside the elegies with his subject so that the poems are as much about his own life as about offering consolation.[2]

Dunn engages with elegy's literariness in the opening poem 'Re-reading Katherine Mansfield's *Bliss and Other Stories*' (E, 9). He establishes a pattern for the book: a combination of underwriting and directly expressed emotion that is prepared to risk sentimentality. The parallel between a fly crushed between the pages of a book in the middle of a story and the poet's wife dead before she was forty is not forced. In contrast, the parallel between the book and the couple's married life is stated directly: 'I flick / Through all our years, my love, and I love you still.' The ending of the poem returns to implication and understatement, focusing on 'this fly, verbosely buried / In "Bliss", one dry tear punctuating "Bliss".' The line also emphasizes that the poems will not bury the life they commemorate with verbosity and become dry, literary tears. In the words of a later poem 'The Stories',

> Why be discreet? A broken heart is what I have –
> A pin to burst the bubble of shy poetry

(E, 58)

Dunn's struggles with literariness continue in 'Tursac', a poem of 'erotic memory' set in France whose remembrances are specifically anti-literary. Dunn calls the couple's house 'our *Thébaïde*' then hears 'her in her best sardonic style: / "Write out of me, not out of what you read"' (E, 26). This is much easier said than written and later poems express deep anxieties about 'my sorrow murdered by aesthetics' (E, 43). 'Tursac' exemplifies what Jacques Derrida, in *The Work of Mourning*, has valuably identified as a process of interiorization which is itself a kind of afterlife: the deceased 'can no longer be but *in us*'.[3] Interiorization as an antidote to literariness is also behind 'Writing with Light' and 'Dining' (E, 23, 27). In the former, Dunn remembers Lesley Dunn's work as a photographer, her fascination with capturing the workings of light or 'the art of day'. At the end of the poem, it is Lesley Dunn who is writing the poems in *Elegies*: 'Writing with light, the heart within my eye / Shines on my grief, my true contemporary'. In 'Dining' Dunn mimics the form and language of classical poetry – 'My lady' – and again commemorates his wife's 'talent to compose the world in light'. The poem takes a different turn when the widowed poet cooks familiar meals with 'old delight / Returning [...] until it feels / As if I have become a woman hidden in me'.[4] Implicitly, the poem writes the poet into what 'Thirteen Steps and the Thirteenth of March' calls the 'conspiracy of women' who helped his wife prepare for death (*E*, 13). The final couplet makes the poem behave like the loved one it remembers and reject the elegiac impulse, refusing 'all grief' and being 'alight / With nature, courage, friendship, appetite'.

'Reading Pascal in the Lowlands' (*E*, 45) suggests that another way out of elegy's literariness is the lives of other people. The poet, sitting reading on a July evening, exchanges a few words with the father of a boy in a wheelchair who is dying of leukaemia. The poem explores reticence as the starting point for what we have seen Dunn describe elsewhere as 'reverence for the real person or event'.[5] The poet doesn't ask the boy's father about the illness. When the father tells Dunn his son has months to live, he is described as 'indiscreet'. The brief conversation makes the poet close his book, the same book that identifies him as 'a stranger', but the poem still implies a kinship between the poet and the boy's father. The lines

> He has seen the limits of time, asking 'Why?'
> Nature is silent on that question.

show the poet recognizing himself in the other man. The last line might also signal a rejection of classical elegies' offering of natural cycles as a source of consolation. At the end of the poem, the poet climbs a hill and looks down on 'A little town, its estuary, its bridge, / Its houses, churches, its undramatic streets.' The effect is to return death and mourning to their proper place in the world as everyday occurrences and unavoidable facts. 'Reading Pascal in the Lowlands' enacts an understanding of the 'terrible bond' of the Registrar's waiting room in 'Arrangements' (*E*, 15) and of the 'truth [...] with its loud grief, / Sensible, commonplace' in 'The Clear Day' (*E*, 40). In the words of another contemporary elegy, Amy Clampitt's 'The Dakota' for John Lennon, 'Grief / is original, but it / repeats itself; there's nothing / more original that it can do.'[6] By the end of the book,

Dunn will be '[sculpting] my foolish poetry / From thwarted life and snapped increase'(*E*, 62).

Elegies gains much of its impact from the way that, as Dave Smith points out, Dunn repeatedly 'makes the poem a contest between language and life' (*RDD*, 89). Nonetheless, despite Dunn's anxieties about both the literariness of elegy and the efficacy of poetry in the face of death, the collection does draw on and benefit from literary antecedents. 'Creatures' (*E*, 33), an evocation of a moment of 'paradisial stasis' in the French countryside, uses ABBA stanzas reminiscent of Tennyson's 'In Memoriam'. The most notable antecedent is the body of poems Thomas Hardy wrote in memory of his first wife Emma.[7] In his study of the modern elegy from Hardy to Heaney, Jahan Ramazani identifies Hardy as a 'transitional' poet in whose work the opposites represented by the hard-won but worthwhile consolation of Tennyson and the sceptical anti-elegies of Geoffrey Hill in our own time 'collide with a special force'.[8] What must be added to Ramazani's account is that this collision is imbricated in Hardy's subject and his treatment of it. Indeed, Melissa F. Zeiger, one of the best critics of modern and contemporary elegy, refers to Dunn specifically to underline how Hardy's importance for later elegists derives from his 'focus on a woman and not a dead male peer, and on a specifically conceived historical woman rather than a mythological personage.'[9] Dunn, then, like Hardy, fills his elegies with doubts, ironies and self-castigations and writes them in a variety of forms. Like Hardy, he sets out to portray a real woman and a real marriage. He also borrows Hardy's central trope of haunting. Lesley Dunn is a 'departing ghost' (*E*, 39), a 'watchful poltergeist' (*E*, 44) and 'a spirit [that] shivers' (*E*, 52). The lines in Hardy's 'The Shadow on the Stone' (*CP*, 498), 'I thought her behind my back / [...] And there was no sound but the fall of the life', are present in Dunn's 'Hush' where 'the first leaves are greening. // Behind me I can hear / A click of fantasy heels, / But there is no one there' (*E*, 63).

Throughout *Elegies*, there are many other references, direct and indirect, to Hardy's poems. Hardy's 'A Circular' (*CP*, 327) in which the poet reads a dress advert sent to his dead wife is paralleled by Dunn's 'Empty Wardrobes' (*E*, 29). 'At Castle Boterel' (*CP*, 330) clearly stands behind Dunn's 'At Cruggleton

Castle' and Hardy's line 'It filled but a minute' can be heard in Dunn's 'Good minutes make good days' (*E*, 31). 'At Castle Boterel' can be heard elsewhere. Hardy's assertion that 'What we did as we climbed, and what we talked of / Matters not much' appears as 'I do not know / Exactly all we talked about or did' in Dunn's 'Chateau d'If' (*E*, 32). Hardy's closing image of a 'phantom figure' seen 'shrinking, shrinking [...] amid the rain' is echoed in Dunn's portrayal of Lesley, in 'Anniversaries', as 'Sweet soul in the athletic rain / And wife now to the weather' (*E*, 59). The shy snake in Dunn's 'Creatures' (*E*, 33) may even be a distant allusion to 'the shy hares' in Hardy's 'The Haunter' (*CP*, 324).

The most important convergence between Hardy's and Dunn's elegies is the movement of each poet between his dead wife's consciousness and his own. This is achieved both directly and indirectly. Unlike Hardy's 'The Haunter', Dunn does not have any poems spoken entirely by his dead wife but there are nine where Lesley Dunn speaks directly. In both sets of elegies we also learn about the dead wives through the imaginative restaging of their inner lives. Hardy's 'A Dream or No' (*CP*, 327) and 'A Death-Day Recalled' (*CP*, 329) tell us of the places that Emma loved and Dunn tells us about Lesley's artistic temperament and sees the objects in the home they made together as embodiments of 'her moments, her secret visions' (*E*, 10). Melissa F. Zeiger's careful reading of Hardy is pertinent here. She notes that the face of the dead wife remembered in 'Your Last Drive' (*CP*, 319) is

> an image of absence alternating with presence, between light and dark, consciousness and death, the imagined and the actual. In this way thinking, reading, writing, and voice, instead of replacing each other in any stable hierarchy, move into a more reciprocal and dynamic relationship – always dependent, of course, on the imagining mind and writing hand of the poet. (Zeiger, 58)

Dunn, of course, unlike Hardy, is not mourning a failed marriage as well as a dead wife. Nonetheless, Zeiger's reading not only helps to illuminate how Dunn's elegiac project is prepared to risk instability but also how that preparedness derives from his abiding concern with reciprocity and responsible looking. There is a definite route from Dunn's observation that in writing *Terry Street* 'I was surrendering to the moods which certain sights and so on were engendering in me' (Haffenden, 17) to his remark on *Elegies* that 'it's reprehensible to talk about an event of such magnitude in terms other than its own' (O'Donoghue, 47). Bernard O'Donoghue, as we have seen, argues that Dunn's early experiments with surrealism and 'enriched language' enable *Elegies* 'to reach the metaphysical heights that helped make it the foremost book of its generation' (*RDD*, 46). Twenty years on, the book's achievements seem much less settled and consistent than such an estimate suggests. *Elegies* is as formally various as any other Dunn collection and this means that some poems are simply less interesting than others.

It is also worth noting that *Elegies* coincided with a powerful elegiac moment in mainstream British poetry. A year before, in 1984, Peter Reading had published *C*, a book length auto-elegy in the persona of a man dying from terminal cancer. *Elegies* was published in the same year as Tony Harrison's anti-elegy *v.* which used the form of Gray's 'Elegy Written in a Country Churchyard'; and Hugo Williams's *Writing Home* elegizing the poet's father.[10] Like Dunn's *Elegies*, all these books are notable for their convergence of elegy and autobiography, that is, the poets place themselves within the elegy and become part of its subject. Elegists are present in canonical elegies such as Milton's 'Lycidas' but their presence is primarily that of the grieving and desiring subject. In these poems of the 1980s, elegy becomes a form of life writing. It is also arguable that the books by Harrison, Reading and Williams are marked by wider social and political changes. Despite the jingoism produced by the Falklands War in 1982, the early 1980s were dominated by such events as the IRA hunger strike in the Maze prison and riots in British cities. Reading's *C* and Harrison's *v.* both portray and lament changes to the civic and industrial fabric of the nation while Williams's *Writing Home* often seems to be elegizing the British mid-century character and experience as much as the poet's father. All three books elegize the passing of the past and even *Elegies* makes an oblique nod in that direction in 'December': 'No friend of ours had ever been to war' (*E*, 53). It may well be that Dunn's work of mourning arrived at a moment when the nation was uniquely ready to receive it.

The final poem of *Elegies*, 'Leaving Dundee', describes the poet setting out for a new life with a new love (*E*, 64). W. N. Herbert notes that 'the city of Dundee makes its first appearance in a book which, for its own tragic reasons, makes [Dunn's] first clear statement of non-engagement' and where he 'emphatically [...] appears as an individual' (*RDD*, 123–4). When Dunn's next collection, *Northlight*, appeared in 1988 he had settled in Tayport across the Firth of Tay with his second wife Lesley (née Bathgate), whom he'd married in 1985, and their baby son Robbie. His primary sources of income were lead book-reviewer for the *Glasgow Herald* and a succession of writer-in-residence posts. The transformation announced by *Elegies*' epigraph from Carducci had become a reality. The opening poem of *Northlight*, 'At Falkland Palace' is dedicated to Lesley but its first lines are evidence that this transformation is poetic as well as personal:

> Innermost dialect
> Describes Fife's lyric hills,
> Life, love and intellect
> In lucid syllables,
> Domestic air.
>
> (*N*, 1)

Inner and outer, thought and feeling, are not just elided but located in each other. The new note is made even clearer by Dunn's use of metres rare in English verse: trimeters followed by a single dimeter. It is equally clear that the 'lucid syllables' carried on these unusual metres exist beyond spoken language and written literature. This idea recurs throughout the first quarter of *Northlight*. A bird's song is 'coincidental literature' in 'S. Frediano's'; a river makes 'white scribbles' in 'The People Before'; and a view of Buddon Ness in 'Daylight' finds 'wordless symposia' and 'luminous discourse' (*N*, 5, 7, 11). 'Going to Aberlemno' involves a journey 'By archaeologies of air' and 'Abernethy' is a place of 'air-psalters', 'pages of stone' and 'leaf libraries' (*N*, 13, 14). This recalls the 'land-language' of 'The Harp of Renfrewshire' (*SKP*, 30) and the 'archeology of hazelraw' in the title poem of *St. Kilda's Parliament* and signals that, as Robert Crawford observes, Dunn's aesthetic is primarily 'archival, despite its surface angers' (*RDD*, 119). However, where those poems mounted counter-histories of dispossession, subsistence and voicelessness, the first twenty pages or so of *Northlight* are decidedly celebratory. In this context, the images of language and literature have two effects. First, they imply that the poems in which they appear are natural extensions of the extra-linguistic and translations of the transient and barely tangible. The collection's concern with naturalness is made clear in the opening poem's description of the world as a 'botanic instrument' – that is, the opposite of horticultural or cultivated – and in six uses of the adjective elsewhere. Second, literary and linguistic images suggest not only that the land itself is a cultural and political resource but also that history can be recovered from other sources than the written record. This is emphasized by the settings of the poems. Falkland Palace is a sixteenth-century house that was the country residence of eight Stuart monarchs, including Mary, Queen of Scots, and the setting for Sir Walter Scott's novel *The Fair Maid of Perth*. Aberlemno is the site of several carved Pictish standing stones and the village of Abernethy, according to the Rev. John Wilson's *Gazetteer of Scotland* (1882), was once 'a capital of Pictavia'.

'At Falkland Palace' introduces other themes. Its middle section portrays 'a posthumous / Nation' but this quickly modulates into something more positive and nourishing. The poet's new life and love and his return to Scotland mean that he is 'bound to history' but in ways that are active and fluid. The next poem 'Love-making by Candlelight' (*N*, 3) elides past and present – as 'At Falkland Palace' elided inner and outer – into an erotic moment that is both 'timeless' and filled with 'rumours from far back'. At the same time, it is a moment of love that enables the poet to say 'sleep, history, sleep.' In 'S. Frediano's' (*N*, 5) we find a Tuscan saint was originally a Scottish missionary so abroad becomes an offshoot of home or, in terms of an opposition explored in a later poem, 'there' turns out to be 'here'. In 'The People Before' (*N*, 7), Scotland is at first a 'post-dated country', language reminiscent of *Barbarians* and *St. Kilda's Parliament*. As in 'Love-making by Candlelight', the poet hears rumours of various pasts but then discovers a place of 'in-betweeness [...] not now, not then' and of 'all death, all birth, / All dying and being reborn'. The same idea is explored in this fine passage from 'Daylight':

> I've seen a star poised on the tip
> Of a still leaf, pure partnership
> Here makes with there and everywhere
> Between life, death and forever.
>
> (N, 12)

In 'Going to Aberlemno' and 'Abernethy' the past becomes audible (N, 13, 14-15). In the former poem, the poet hears 'A Pictish dialect / [...] [cry] / For lyric nationhood' and, in the latter, the present is a Dark Age herdsman's 'aftermath' in a scene lit by 'Northlight's late druidic rinse'. 'Rinse' – like 'dust' – is a word that does special work in Dunn's œuvre. Here, as in 'Winter Graveyard' and 'The Harp of Renfrewshire' – from *Love or Nothing* and *St. Kilda's Parliament* respectively – its mingled meanings of cleansing and changing colour have the dual effect of reinforcing the transitoriness of a moment and registering the poet's own care and reverence in capturing that transitoriness.

Dunn's subject in the first part of *Northlight* is perhaps nothing less than immanence itself. The poems are almost ceremonial acts devoted to the permanent abodes of inner activating forces or spirits. There are references to the 'mystic Firth' (N, 19) and to 'mystic lights' reflected in the Tay (N, 22). It seems as if the poet has given himself up totally to what he described to John Haffenden as 'the play of phenomena and experience' (Haffenden 23) and is ready to go on imagining 'the estuary of dream'. Then, in 'Broughty Ferry', Dunn checks himself and reminds us that 'I won't disfigure loveliness I see / With an avoidance of its politics' and that 'I think of incomes and prosperity' (N, 24). The next poem 'Here and There' tests this secure self-knowledge against how his new life appears to others. Twelve twelve-line rhymed stanzas quietly but insistently rebuff criticisms from an English friend. Dunn is 'provincial' with 'literature and a career to lose'; has turned '[his] back on history'; and 'serves a lowered will with local song, / Beachcombing an iambic neighbourhood' (N, 30). Dunn's answers show that the relationship of the personal and the historical has been realigned. Tayport is, he asserts,

> Trebizond
> As easily as a regenerate
> Country in which to reconstruct a self

> From local water, timber, light and earth.
>
> (N, 26)

Scotland, specifically Tayport, is 'love's preferred country' where, at the end of the poem, the poet sees

> Plurals and distances in voiceless wet
> Enough to harbour all my history
> Inside a house protected from regret.
>
> (N, 30)

The realignment of the personal and the historical comes from the new perspective gained from living on 'imagination's waterfronts'. It is a perspective that not only enables Dunn to dismiss his critic's Englishness as 'an undignified anachronism' – a term applied to historical legacies in two earlier poems in *Northlight* – but, more importantly, allows him to redefine what Englishness identifies as provincial. Tayport is not a backwater but a place where the quotidian converges with the 'speculative spirit which is midwife / To nation, intellect and poetry's / Occurrence.' The implication that the margin originates the centre sharpens the echo in the poem's title of Philip Larkin's 'Here' which, in the words of Sean O'Brien, 'seems to gesture at some missing term for affirmation or acceptance or assumption into the non-human elements.'[11] 'Here and There' distances itself from English provincialism as does the similarly modified albeit distant echo of Larkin's '"Nothing, like something, happens anywhere"' in 'Love-making by Candlelight's' evocation of 'our private anywhere'. The next poem in *Northlight* is, appropriately, Dunn's fine elegy for Philip Larkin 'December's Door' (N, 31) which like 'Stranger's Grief', the elegy for Robert Lowell in *Barbarians*, uses a leaf to evoke passing and survival (B, 51–2). 'A church leaf', withering in the 'printed air' of a book, is 'sorrow's vernacular' with a 'secret value / A matter of downtrodden poetry'. The poem's evocation of trees, woods and night are distant but clear allusions to the general scene in Gray's 'Elegy Written in a Country Churchyard' as 'unknown tree' is to Gray's 'fav'rite tree'. The combination of vernacular and classical is typical of Dunn's later work. The poem's last line, 'Remote, unswept oblivions', cleverly evokes the unfulfilled transcendental yearnings of Larkin's poetry by mimicking his unusual negatives. This poem too views its subject from the perspective of Tayport and Budden Ness. When Dunn writes 'And now I can't repay the debt I owe' it is hard, in the light of the previous poem, not to read beyond the immediate reason of Larkin's death and hear a further statement of Dunn's poetic distance from England and from his mentor.

The next thirty or so pages of *Northlight* turn aside from the arguments opened and explored in the book's first fourteen poems. After their cumulative re-imaginings of self and nation, Dunn clearly felt able to relax and offer what is largely – with the exception of an elegy for John Brogan (*N*, 52) and an evocation of the early life of Edwin Muir (*N*, 37) – a collection of entertainments, travelogues and reminiscences. 'Winkie', for example, devotes nearly 100 lines to the wartime adventures of a pigeon now in a glass case in a Dundee museum; and 'In the 1950s' gives a similar space to a fictionalized account of the advent of television (*N*, 33, 47). Such poems are never less than entertaining and readable but, in the context of the beautiful and subtle writing that precedes them, it is hard not to feel they are too occasional and too relaxed. Indeed, lines like 'He didn't say if it was the hand of a man or a woman' from 'The War in the Congo' cannot be called poetry by even the slackest measure of free verse (*N*, 50). Dunn's response to such criticism would no doubt be that, in the words of 'Here and There', poems such as 'Maggie's Corner', 'Running the East Wind' and 'Jig of the Week No.21' '[serve] loyalty [...] / [...] responsibility and caprice' (*N*, 54, 55, 43).

The closing section of *Northlight* includes three powerful poems that re-examine the collection's central themes: 'The Dark Crossroads', 'Memory and Imagination' and 'Adventure's Oafs' (*N*, 62, 65, 80). 'Memory and Imagination', originally written to accompany an exhibition at the Royal Scottish Academy, Edinburgh, returns to the mystical sense of timelessness explored in the collection's opening poems. The poem's lovely extended lyric records what Dunn would later describe in his 1990 interview with *The Printer's Devil* as 'previously unfamiliar dimensions of reality [...] spiritual experiences which are quotidian, everyday, commonplace' (PD, 27). 'Metre's continuum' elides with 'the river's tidal pulse' and gives access to 'the visionary and its sacrament' and 'imagination's second sight'. The view over Buddon Ness turns into 'the inside-out of

Caledonia's / Cognitive acres stripped of time and laws' and 'self's transformed / Into its anonym'. This celebration of loss of self comes after 'The Dark Crossroads', a poem where the self is constrained by the misprisions of other people. Sean O'Brien observes that both 'The Dark Crossroads' and 'Adventure's Oafs' 'deal with occasions when the atlas of possibilities imagined from Scotland is unacknowledged' (*RDD*, 78). 'The Dark Crossroads' finds Dunn at the dark heart of Englishness's 'undignified anachronism': an English pub of 'fossilized, sinister gaiety' in which 'Five words have uttered who I am and where / I come from [...] / [...] their false Scotland'. Dunn nurses his pint in a corner while another drinker does impersonations of Scotsmen that the poet is meant to hear. The last quarter of the poem is a guilty, rather half-hearted 'notional revenge' and 'library carnage'. Dunn stands 'in fine rain watching dust curdle', an image that harks back to *Terry Street* where dust was a metonym for a way of life that had become petrified through the disregard of those living it. The poem may attempt to rise above the offence by dismissing the poet's response as 'obsolete signals / Describing a defensive hate' but the overall impression is of exhausted resignation to the fact that England and Scotland will always relate to each other via racist stereotypes. 'Adventure's Oafs' uses a Territorial Army exercise to portray Scotland as an occupied country ruled by a government only 'a quarter voted for' with 'the mighty X', a phrase which sounds like a wish for proportional representation. The poem wonders 'What's absolute in nations? No one knows...' but finds that only 'Occult History' has the answer: 'It's yesterday [...] / You're colonized! Maybe you didn't know?' (*N*, 81).

Northlight ends, therefore, as a much more political book than its opening poems suggested. The hope expressed at the end of 'Love-making by Candlelight' that history might sleep has proved impossible. The distance between the book's opening word, the Hopkinsian 'innermost', and its closing one 'infamous' underlines this. Dunn's sense of responsibility means he cannot avoid the politics at work on 'love's preferred country' and has to register growing Scottish anger at Tory rule from Westminster. 'Adventure's Oafs' highlights what Cairns Craig sees as 'the sense of an achieved – and threatened – communality' although it must be pointed out that a sense of threat is absent from much of the book and that communality is largely between individual and locale.[12] The communality of 'Maggie's Corner' (*N*, 54), 'In the 1950s' (*N*, 47) and 'The Departures of Friends in Childhood' (*N*, 61) is set firmly in the past. Indeed, while there is a strong sense of literal ground ready to express its democratic spirit into what a poem in *Love or Nothing* named 'The Estuarial Republic' it is a republic often seeming to comprise only the poet or the poet and his family. Nonetheless, the political crisis caused by the Poll Tax – introduced in Scotland in 1989 – would lead Dunn to write the *Counterblast* pamphlet *Poll Tax: The Fiscal Fake* (1990) in which he observes that,

> From north of border England once again looks the way George Orwell described it, 'a land of snobbery and privilege, ruled largely by the old and silly'. No, England is not like that; it just looks like it. (*PT*, 30)

The pamphlet also includes the poem 'Poor People's Cafés' which anatomizes 'this lowered / Epoch' and 'this hurt land' in which 'it grows late / For the decencies'. The opening poems of *Northlight* viewed history as an ever-present pastness which could, nonetheless, be put to sleep with love. Its closing poem, like 'Poor People's Cafés', recognizes that actions in the present ensure history remains sleepless.

5

Decencies, Disenchantments and Diversity

Despite Dunn's characterization of the 1990s as 'this lowered epoch', the decade got off to a happy and productive start for him personally. In 1990, his daughter Lillias was born and he received a Cholmondeley Award; and in 1991 he was appointed Professor of English Literature at the University of St. Andrews. The opening years of the decade also saw the publication of *Poll Tax: The Fiscal Fake* and of his translation, in rhyming couplets, of Racine's *Andromache* which was originally commissioned for a BBC Radio 3 production. He was also busy as an editor: *The Essential Browning*, *Scotland: An Anthology* and *The Faber Book of Twentieth-Century Scottish Poetry* all appeared between 1990 and 1992.

We have already noted Dunn's equation of poetry with national identity in his Introduction to the Faber book. Similar questions – whether Scotland is a nation or the Nothing identified by Edwin Muir, how a regenerate nation can come from Nothing – dominate a significant proportion of his 1993 collection *Dante's Drum-kit*. However, the most immediately striking thing about the book is its zesty productivity. At 129 pages, it is his most substantial collection. It comprises five sections and several lengthy sequences including 'Disenchantments' which meditates on the after-life and literary posterity; and 'Dressed to Kill' which was originally commissioned for the BBC2 television series *Words on Film*. The first section of the book finds Dunn in expansive comic mode. 'Academy's Runners' (*DDK*, 3–5); 'Turn Over a New Leaf' (*DDK*, 6–7), a swipe at millennial anxieties; a review in verse of Henry Petroski's *The Pencil: A History* (*DDK*, 9–10); and 'Kabla Khun' (*DDK*, 11–15) – in which Coleridge attempts to get his revenge on The Person from Porlock – use either couplets or ABAB rhyming stanzas and many use long, anapaestic lines of 12–14 syllables. All are examples of what W. N. Herbert has identified as 'the destabilising element' in Dunn's comedy that relies on a marriage of formalism and surrealism (*RDD*, 133). Dunn may sometimes cross over into William McGonagall territory but it's clear he's enjoying himself. The group includes 'Libraries. A Celebration' (*DDK*, 18-20) which contains an incisive vignette of

> my old boss, Philip Larkin, holding a book
> Written in Indonesian, published in Djarkata,
> As if it were a toad that spoke back to him, saying,
> 'Isn't it *wonderful*? That someone understands *this*?
>
> (*DDK*, 19)

As we might expect with Dunn, characteristic concerns surface in the light verse. For example, the poem-review of Henry Petroski's book recommends it as a lesson 'that life's a perpetual quest / For what can be decently made, and then improved' (*DDK*, 10) and looks forward to the question asked in the 'Disenchantments' sequence 'What has a decent poetry left to teach?' (*DDK*, 37). We have seen that Dunn characterizes it as the 'ethic' of 'remote communities' (Crawford, 26) and a way of looking. Decency is also presumably behind these lines from 'Bagni di Lucca', an Italian-set meditation on the life and work of Elizabeth Barrett Browning:

> What should we do, other than write, sing, praise
> The best in life and us, and being brave
> With what we have, and what we do not have?
>
> (*DDK*, 23)

Other poems in the first part of *Dante's Drum-kit* revisit themes familiar from *Northlight* and elsewhere. 'Australian Dream-Essay' (*DDK*, 25–27), a paean to Australia and the poet Les Murray, finds that 'there' is once again an extension of 'here' but with the possibility that origins don't get in the way of 'a deserved identity'. 'Bedfordshire' (*DDK*, 16–17) reads like an updated version of 'A Poem in Praise of the British' with its image of a nation in a state of political torpor.

The second part of *Dante's Drum-kit* is devoted to 'Disenchantments' (*DDK*, 31–46). The nine-part sequence is in nearly 130 stanzas of *terza rima*, the verse form which Dunn calls

'Dante's drum-kit'. The verse is chatty, quick-footed and further evidence of Dunn's belief in the happy co-existence of the classical and the vernacular. The sequence offers extended reflections on the after-life but, just as importantly, it amounts to a cumulative clarification of Dunn's post-*Elegies* view of his art that offers an implicit answer to the question of what a decent poetry has left to teach. The quotidian spiritual dimension familiar from *Northlight* and called here 'the transfigured commonplace' (*DDK*, 33) is the ground of Dunn's meditations. The dead appear only in 'life's interior extra sense' and the hereafter 'happens in the eye and intellect'. (*DDK*, 32, 34) Also familiar from *Northlight* is section IV's portrayal of Scotland as the presence of the past: 'nothing on the eye other than bygones', all viewed with an 'untimed lucidity' (*DDK*, 35, 37). It is this lucidity that allows Dunn to reject various visions of the afterlife in favour of one that is 'pagan, please, Republican, / Domestic, set in very private grounds // A spacious grave where all five senses quicken' (*DDK*, 38, 40). The poem ends with the assertion that 'If there's an afterlife, it's in the mind / Of anyone who thinks about the dead' and that once you have accepted the ghosts that live in your head '*that's* when you own / Your miserable life entirely' (*DDK*, 44, 45). The sequence ends with an instruction to 'Look to the living, love them, and hold on' (*DDK*, 46).

The relationship between the living and the dead, the acceptance of ghosts and the ownership of life are the subjects of most of the eleven poems that comprise part III of *Dante's Drum-kit* but in the context of nation. *Northlight* portrayed Scotland as a country both lacking and denied substantial written histories but still possessing a past recoverable from extra-linguistic resources. Part III of *Dante's Drum-kit* imagines the people who might have contributed to its lost histories and the people who inhabit it now. The picture is a bleak one for poems such as 'Moorlander', 'The Crossroads of the Birds', "Bare Ruined Choirs", 'The Penny Gibbet', 'Gaberlunzie' and 'Nineteen-Thirteen' portray a country of beggars, vagrants and industrial working-class subsistence (*DDK*, 49, 52, 54, 56, 57, 58). The eponymous moorlander is 'downwind of [...] civilization'; the protagonist of 'The Crossroads of the Birds' is a blind beggar 'ancestral and orthodox'; and even the title month of 'Queen February' is a 'malevolent waif' (*DDK*, 83). The extra-linguistic is also the extra-communal. It is no surprise to find a sudden preponderance of Larkinesque negatives: 'unrecorded' and 'unresolved' both appear more than once as well as more unusual coinages such as 'unhappened Homer' and language that is 'unbegged, unsold'. In Dunn's first three collections such words focused a profoundly unillusioned gaze but here they insist on cultural, economic and political dispossession. They are terms that are, in the words of 'The Local' from *St. Kilda's Parliament*, 'hopelessly in touch' with what they describe.

The first six poems of Part III are all set in the past and, as with the largely unpopulated poems of place in *Northlight*, risk portraying Scotland as an 'anachronism'. It is a recurrent term in that book and in *Dante's Drum-kit* but the next three poems – 'Body Echoes', 'Swigs' and 'Poor People's Cafés' reprinted from *Poll Tax: The Fiscal Fake* – show that Dunn is doing more than writing reparative histories (*DDK*, 60, 65, 76). 'Body Echoes' portrays a man and a woman – 'national halves' – who are versions of characters another contemporary Scottish poem by Kathleen Jamie calls Mr. and Mrs. Scotland. They both 'shed the present tense / To reconstruct a monstrous permanence' because the 'past and present are unreconciled' (*DDK*, 61, 62). They live in

> an unrecorded country that
> Historians don't know of. If they do
> They fear its absence of modernity,
> Its unresolved remorse...
>
> (*DDK*, 61–2)

Dunn's Mr. and Mrs. Scotland are physical throwbacks trapped in historically determined behaviours that mean 'They don't, and didn't, give enough to life' (*DDK*, 64). Scotland is not only a country where it is easy to live in the past but also one where national characteristics are [hobbling] the future. 'Swigs', a twelve part sequence, uses various views of 'old drunks' to probe the state of the nation. Dunn is 'ashamed / Of my country' and in section VI observes that 'It went away, but now / It's all come back again. / These men are my age, though...' (*DDK*, 66, 68). The final section remembers drunks, exotic and romantic, Dunn saw when he was a boy and throws into sharper relief that the preceding sections have been anatomizing not just drunkenness but a symptom of national impoverishment.

However, in the midst of all this, Dunn inserts a moment of apparent pastoral retreat and reflection. 'Weeding a Border' rejects the idea that Scotland can be described purely in terms of a 'land-language' of unrecorded dispossession. The gardener contemplates

> – Respublica; république; la chose publique:
> Difficult issues steeped in mellow life's
> Agreeable distractions, our words causing
> Stammering embarrassment, unable to prise free
> Beauty, bird-song, preferable politics.
>
> (*DDK*, 59)

In one's garden, it's possible to feel like a citizen and believe in a direct route between 'mellow' and 'preferable'. The surrounding poems portray what causes that 'stammering embarrassment' and postpones the future.

'Audenesques for 1960', the first poem of Part IV, introduces another change of mood (*DDK*, 89–91). The poem recalls the young poet's imaginary conversations with the older poet whom he saw 'once only, on the other side of a room' and was too shy to talk to. The poem is partly a portrait of the artist as a young man but, more importantly, it is as if after a group of poems addressed primarily to a Scottish readership and to the condition of Scotland, Dunn feels obliged to advertise his membership of an international brotherhood of poets. He regrets that other people's 'national distrust' made him keep quiet about Auden's influence. He goes on to assert that 'Muses are international'; that he speaks English 'But not its nationality'; and that 'imagination side-steps / Half-witted nagging about "National Identity"' (*DDK*, 91). There is, however, something a little over-insistent about the repetitions as if Dunn doesn't quite believe what he is saying. The poem ends rather abruptly looking out over the 'wordless calm' of the Firth but sets the scene for what follows as Part IV gives a series of reports from 'mellow life'. 'Audenesques' describes Dunn as 'Pushing fifty' and several poems – 'One Thing and Another', 'Early Autumn', 'A Game of Bowls' and 'Middle Age' – describe midlife as new awareness of both the present and of the relationship of the past to the present. Just as Scotland is imagined as an extra-linguistic and extra-communal place so this new awareness and the past become unnamable. In one poem, the past 'feels like a half-tune / You can't put a name to'; and in another the poet searches fruitlessly for the grave of a childhood friend's pet (*DDK*, 97, 102–103). 'Just Standing There', ostensibly about a local wooden bridge, links these experiences to the quotidian spiritual. 'Reality' is

> [...] a precise spot of nowhere and timelessness
> Within myself, a door I can go through and be invisible
> In a room also invisible or from which I come back
> Without memory other than the languageless noise in the ears
>
> (*DDK*, 101)

Poetry may begin with languageless noise and life in Tayport may help the poet to hear it more clearly but the poet's own position is less certain. Dunn began *The Happier Life* with 'The Garden' whose first words were 'Neighbours hate it...' In 'Preserve and Renovate' he is still trying to bed himself down in suburbia (*DDK*, 95-6). A neighbour, busy at 'The kirky vision of his husbandry', becomes a subject of contemplation on the poet's daily walk, not least because he looks like his late father. The poem is not, however, an elegy but a meditation on Dunn's vocation. The work of poetry is 'this risk of feeling, that the sweet and true / Might be preserved' and comes from

> obedience to
> Time and experience, for what is due
> To being, to be life's accomplice.
>
> (*DDK*, 96)

There is an unstable mixture of satisfaction and self-pity in the movement of these lines which presumably derives from a recurrent anxiety for male poets of Dunn's age and class – that poetry must somehow be made, or at least felt to be, equivalent to real work.

Dante's Drum-kit ends with 'Dressed to Kill', a rhyming sequence about Scottish regiments' role in the British Empire. As John Bayley noted in a contemporary review, the poem makes 'the best possible use of a national sense and sentiment, which is quite disenchanted and absolutely sterling into the bargain'.[1] The most interesting aspect, in terms of the collection and Dunn's other books from *Barbarians* onwards, is the ending:

> *The Thin Red Line* above a mantelpiece
> Defeats my pacifism, and strikes me dumb –
> [...]
> Ironic sepoy. *Whaash my nashun?*
> No answer. Silence's oration.
>
> (*DDK*, 145)

The question echoes Seamus Heaney's use of MacMorris's question 'What ish my nation?' from Shakespeare's *Henry V* in his poem 'Traditions'.[2] Heaney describes the question as whingeing and has it answered 'sensibly, though so much later' by 'the wandering Bloom' from Joyce's *Ulysses* "Ireland". Dunn's silence, read back into the collection, suggests that Scotland has yet to find an answer it is comfortable with.

In the interview given to Attila Dösa in 1999, Dunn says that he has become increasingly wary of the political dimension of his writing: 'I hope that the "act of imagination" is more conspicuous in my recent work' (Dösa, 33). His next book, the verse novel *The Donkey's Ears*, finds Dunn still trying to strike a balance between the distractions of politics and the imperatives of the imagination. The book began life as a commission from the Ferens Art Gallery in Hull in 1983 for an exhibition called 'The Day the Russian Imperial Fleet Fired on the Hull Trawlermen'. The attack – known locally as the Dogger Bank Incident – occurred in 1905 as the Russian fleet was on an improbable round the world voyage to attack the Japanese navy. The Russians were defeated in the battle of Tsushima sometimes called the Trafalgar of the East. In Japanese Tsushima means 'the Donkey's Ears' and refers to twin peaks on an island near the site of the battle. The book's title also inevitably alludes to King Midas who was given ass's ears by Apollo – a mark of stupidity and lack of judgment. The 'Author's Note' tells us Dunn published what would be the first part of *The Donkey's Ears* in *Encounter* in 1983 and added bits over the years before 'returning to it "full time" in 1997: Partly this was due to an abhorrence of leaving a piece of work unfinished. Also, I felt an instinctive need to write a poem about the twentieth century' (*TDE*, 175).

Dunn's persistence produced a nine part verse novel made up of 120 cantos of anywhere between two and seventeen quatrains. Dunn's narrator is Flag Engineer Eugène Sigismondovitch Politovsky who perished in the battle and Dunn draws on his letters home to his wife Sophie which were published posthumously. Dunn makes Politovsky a poet in order to explain how his letters are in verse. Dunn told Robert Crawford that he was drawn to the geographical sweep of the original letters – from the North Sea to the Korea Strait with many tropical stops in between: 'The French African colonies in 1904–1905 – fascinating! Pictorializing these things is, I find, an interesting source of poetic imagery'. (Crawford, 33). Dunn also told Crawford that he saw Politovsky as 'essentially civilian, but wrapped in this gigantic naval enterprise' (Crawford, 33) so it's inevitable that part of the story of *The Donkey's Ears* is history itself. History, as we might expect from Dunn's earlier books, is a combination of ill-advised adventuring ('colossal pointlessness' – *TDE*, 79), irresistible forces ('I think it is the century compels us' – *TDE*, 9) and quotidian realities. Politovsky tells Sophie and us that 'Discomfort is the stuff of history' (*TDE*, 5) and that 'History's // a matter of [...] boring details' (*TDE*, 90).

Another strand in *The Donkey's Ears* is modernity. The word recurs throughout Politovsky's letters and is one sign of Dunn's need to write something about the twentieth century. Politovsky equates modernity with carnage and destruction: 'Modernity's made slaughter out of warfare' he tells us and later imagines it having a 'door that leads to Hell' (*TDE*, 44, 161). The battle of Tsushima comes to stand for a century of similar disasters resulting from a failure to understand modernity or at any rate the speed of historical change. Politovsky allows Dunn to give free play to the dyspeptic strain in his poetry but an engineer-poet is also an ideal persona for a writer who once wrote his poems 'should be Clyde-built, crude and sure [...] A poetry of nuts and bolts'. The persona of Politovsky allows Dunn to avoid the anxiety expressed in his earlier work and in the poetry of contemporaries like Tony Harrison and Seamus Heaney over whether poetry is proper work for men. An engineer-poet also goes some way to disarming criticism of the poetry. Dunn told Crawford that most of Politovsky's letters 'are very dull and [he], I think, probably was a dull man, but I'll have to make him [...] into someone who was interesting' (Crawford, 33). As this suggests, there are a number of difficulties with the writing. First, the shape of the narrative is an awkward one. Parts One to Four have a definite pace and set the shipboard scene well.

However, Part Five describing a lengthy stop in Madagascar is overlong at thirty-nine cantos; and the final four parts often seem to repeat the overall mood of the opening four. *The Donkey's Ears* is a journey without a destination. Second, much of what Dunn has to describe is how an individual deals with claustrophobic boredom and events aboard ship hold little interest for readers not already fascinated by the sea.

Finally, although Dunn tells us he rarely departed from Politovsky's letters, the voice of *The Donkey's Ears* is recognizably Dunn especially in its commentating on modernity and imperialism. The effect is similar to countless film and television adaptations of classic novels where historical characters are translated into modern people in fancy dress and the audience is titillated with the knowingness of hindsight. One leaves *The Donkey's Ears* admiring its dogged achievement but feeling that both a more interesting character and better-known events would have given Dunn richer material with which to dramatize the conflict between the imagination and its distractions.

Reviewing Dunn's most recent collection *The Year's Afternoon*, published in 2000, for the *TLS*, Gerald Mangan noted 'a sense of intimacy in the writing that is not always comfortable'.[3] The collection starts and finishes in the poet's garden with celebrations of leisure and daydreaming – 'The Year's Afternoon' and 'Indolence' (*TYE*, 3–5, 79–81) – and a reference to 'my instinctive, field-sized republic' suggests we can expect to find Dunn in Horatian mode. However, the mood of the book seems largely determined by the break-up of Dunn's second marriage and his new life alone in Dairsie, a place he told Attila Dösa is 'smaller even than Tayport' (Dösa, 31). *The Year's Afternoon* is full of insomniac night watches, silence and solitude: 'in the cold dark at 2 a.m.', 'late-night silence', 'a domesticity of one' and 'accessories of solitude' are typical phrases. Towards the end of the book Dunn foresees Mangan's concerns. In '*Bête Noire's* Edition of *Terry Street* with Photographs by Robert Whitaker' (*TYE*, 69-73) he '[speaks] with a full heart, conscious of believing in what is best' and adds that 'if this is close to the unbearably intimate / Then allow me, at least, to call it my poem'. *The Year's Afternoon* is certainly Dunn's most personal and nakedly emotional collection since *Elegies*. It is also the most downbeat of all his books because it lacks one of their essential components: dreams of a better future. Dunn is not the first person to have discovered that the single life turns the gaze inwards and backwards. The Terry Street poem is one of several pieces of unhappy retrospection. 'On Whether Loneliness Ever Has a Beginning' reminisces on past loves but ends in a present where 'solitude blows back' from the end of the poet's garden and 'There is colossal silence. / It is my silence. / It comes from me' (*TYE*, 48–56: 54). In 'Woodnotes' the poet sees his double in a wood and 'abject but happy' sniffs 'the stink of my remorse / Flow[ing] from my years and deeds' (*TYE*, 38–40: 38). Indeed, where Dunn's poetry is predominantly optical, *The Year's Afternoon* is his most olfactory collection. Smells and perfumes recur and, in the context of 'the stink', it is notable that several poems use 'fragrance' to describe something that is desired but unobtainable.

If the lines from '*Bête Noire*'s Edition of *Terry Street*...' seem to be pleading for emotion to be made poetry without too much work, many poems in the book seem to have little more than scorn for the work of poetry. 'Pushkin's Ring' – a faction about what happened to the poet's ring after it was stolen from the Pushkin Museum in 1917 – connects this with Dunn's divorce and confesses he has lost his wedding ring 'Because of poetry, being married to it' (*TYE*, 44–6: 46). Different poems call poetry 'small', 'lonely' (on three separate occasions), 'pathetic and pious', 'clumsy', 'lies' and 'consolations of shame and averted perfection'. 'Leopardi', addressed to the Italian poet Dunn has translated, cannot quite bring itself to be the affirmation of poetry it so clearly wants to be (*TYE*, 41–3). Poetry is an art 'submerged / In its reviled soil of self and famished / Desires' and the poet speaks to Leopardi 'across the years from my own sickness'. (*TYE*, 42)

Poetry's involvement with abjection and its ability to access what *Elegies* called 'the sob in the intellect' are clearly behind Dunn's many uses of the word 'cry'. The deaths of Norman MacCaig, Sorley MacLean and George Mackay Brown in 'Three Poets' (*TYE*, 32–6) are 'a tripled cry' and in 'Leopardi' poetry is 'a lyric cry'. At the same time the poems in *The Year's Afternoon* want such cries to be heard for what they are. In 'On Whether Loneliness Ever Has a Beginning' the poet lives in 'my mouthless silence' where 'I listen to my own cry' and 'East Riding' – about a return to Hull – concludes that 'Recalcitrant, /

All life can make is its domestic cry' (*TYE*, 55, 68). Finally, in '*Bête Noire*'s Edition of *Terry Street*...' Dunn asserts that he still possesses 'the same idealism, an indestructible cry / Persevering despite what happens' (*TYE*, 71–2).

The Year's Afternoon is, then, not an easy book to read but it is certainly a brave one to have written. It attests to what 'Out of Breath' calls 'A will to survive without self-pity or – parody' and is often prepared to risk both (*TYE*, 63). The book is not exclusively devoted to remorseful confession and self-examination. Dunn does not neglect what 'Teachers' call 'my lyric care' for 'The indefinite and infinite' and there are some lovely moments (*TYE*, 28). 'Parsing this silence is listening to wood', for example, or the 'solitary star' whose 'displaced radiance is caught by a daisy. / It is a tear of drinkable dew' (*TYE*, 60, 21). What is perhaps most striking about *The Year's Afternoon* is that it manages to be one of Dunn's most tonally and texturally consistent collections. All the poems read as if he felt genuinely moved to write them as opposed to obeying a sense of responsibility to social and political distractions not of his invention.

Dunn's wish to avoid 'self-parody' also came up in the interview with Attila Dösa and he added that 'At my age [...] it's a good idea to try to stay new, if it can be managed [...] having published a book, I somehow, without deliberating it, make sure that the next book is different from its predecessor' (Dösa, 32–3). The last line of *The Year's Afternoon* looks forward to a range of things of which 'Not one means work' and other poems talk about 'ambitionlessness' and doing nothing except attending to 'something in me that insists it sings / Freely' (*TYE*, 65). With this in mind, it seems right to let the poet himself have the last word on his future career:

> My Muse demands of me that I have room for anything at all, for everything, the erotic and lyrical, the topical and political, the discursive and autobiographical, the main theme and the absolutely digressive, the very significant and the nursery rhyme. If there's anything I want as a poet, it's the stamina to maintain diversity and the response to what's necessary for my circumstances of writing.
>
> (Dösa, 34)

Notes

PREFACE

1. 'From the Lost Ground: Liz Lochhead, Douglas Dunn and Contemporary Scottish Poetry', in Acheson, James and Romana Huk, eds., *Contemporary British Poetry: Essays in Theory and Criticism* (Albany: State University of New York Press, 1996), 343–372: 360–70.
2. King, Charles and Iain Crichton Smith, eds., *Twelve More Modern Scottish Poets* (London: Hodder and Stoughton, 1986), 116.
3. *English Poetry since 1940*, 154–5.
4. 'Young Women in Rollers', *TS*, 29–30; and *N*, 30 and 25.
5. Gregson, Ian, '"There are many worlds": The 'Dialogic' in Terry Street and After', in *Reading Douglas Dunn*, ed. by Robert Crawford and David Kinloch (Edinburgh: Edinburgh University Press, 1992), 17–31: 25.
6. For a fuller discussion of gender in *Terry Street*, see my "What does the fairy DO?" The Staging of Antithetical Masculine Styles in the poetry of Tony Harrison and Douglas Dunn', *Textual Practice* 14.1 (2000), 115–136.
7. Email correspondence with the author, 05.12.05.
8. Remark in a talk about his work, given at 'Cultural Identities: A Symposium on Contemporary British & Irish Poetry, University of Łódź, Poland, 13 May 2003.
9. O'Brien, Sean, 'Douglas Dunn: Ideology and Pastoral' in *The Deregulated Muse* (Newcastle upon Tyne: Bloodaxe Books, 1998), 65–80: 77.
10. 'Importantly Live', edited version in *Bloodaxe Critical Anthologies: Tony Harrison*, 254.
11. Heaney, Seamus, *Seeing Things* (London: Faber and Faber, 1991), 78.
12. Campbell, Ian, *Kailyard: A New Assessment* (Edinburgh: The Ramsay Head Press, 1981), 113.
13. *Seamus Heaney and the Language of Poetry* (London: Harvester

Wheatsheaf, 1994), 61.
14. Hechter, Michael, *Internal Colonialism: The Celtic Fringe in English National Development 1536–1966* (London: Routledge & Kegan Paul, 1975), 342.
15. Ibid., 257.
16. Email correspondence with the author, 05.12.05.
17. Michael Hechter, 342.
18. 'Formal Strategies in Tony Harrison's Poetry, in Neil Astley, ed., *Bloodaxe Critical Anthologies 1: Tony Harrison* (Newcastle upon Tyne: Bloodaxe Books, 1991), 129–132: 129.
19. O'Brien, Sean, 'Douglas Dunn: Ideology and Pastoral' in *The Deregulated Muse* (Newcastle upon Tyne: Bloodaxe Books, 1998), 65–80: 65.
20. 'Pleasures of Invention, Rigours of Responsibility: Some notes on the poetry of Douglas Dunn', *PN Review*, Volume 10, Number 2 (1983), 43–46.
21. 'Haunted by each other', *TLS*, April 25 2003, 13.
22. Useful introductions to Dunn's short stories and criticism can be found in the *Reading Douglas Dunn* volume. See, respectively, Anne Varty, 'Telling Short Stories', 138–150; and Richard Price, 'Taking Exception: Douglas Dunn's Criticism', 168–181.

CHAPTER ONE

1. Raban, Jonathan, *The Society of the Poem* (London: Harrap, 1971), 70.
2. See, respectively, 'Maiden Name', 'Triple Name' and 'I Remember, I Remember' in *Collected Poems* (London: Faber & Faber, 1988), 101, 73 and 81.
3. Raban, op. cit.
4. Williams, Raymond, *Culture and Society 1780-1950* (London: Chatto & Windus, 1958), 325.
5. However, it is important not to miss other dimensions to the poem. In the version of the poem that appears in the 1986 *Selected Poems* 'my softness' is changed to 'my culture' which serves to simplify the poem into a conventional class narrative of low and high culture, real life and art. The original adds a gender anxiety to anxiety about the relation between class origin and the destinations made possible by education. Dunn's 'softness' means that he will never acquire the god-like invisibility of the 'Men of Terry Street' and he worries that he perhaps has more in common with its women. What the women appear to mock, then, is not just Dunn's high culture but his apparent lack of conventional masculinity.
6. Quoted in Neil Corcoran, *English Poetry since 1940* (Harlow:

Longman, 1993), 87.
7. See *RDD*, 72; and Cairns Craig, 'From the Lost Ground: Liz Lochhead, Douglas Dunn and Contemporary Scottish Poetry', in Acheson, James and Romana Huk, eds., *Contemporary British Poetry: Essays in Theory and Criticism* (Albany: State University of New York Press, 1996), 343–372. op.cit., 344–6.
8. *English Poetry since 1940* (Harlow: Longman, 1993), 93.

CHAPTER TWO

1. See, respectively, Lindsay quoted in Haffenden interview, 20; and Alan Robinson, *Instabilities in Contemporary British Poetry* (Basingstoke: Macmillan, 1988), 87–88
2. See Dunn's interview with *The Printer's Devil*, 23–4, for a fuller account of Larkin's editorial involvement.
3. Peter Jones and Michael Schmidt, eds., *British Poetry since 1970: a critical survey* (Manchester: Carcanet, 1980), ix.
4. I am here indebted to Robert Hewison, *Too Much: Art and Society in the Sixties 1960–1975* (London: Methuen, 1988), 226–271 and his fuller account.
5. Remark in a talk about his poetry given at 'Cultural Identities: A Symposium on Contemporary British & Irish Poetry', University of Łódź, 13 May 2003.
6. Both the Porter and Andrews reviews are quoted on the jacket of *Barbarians*.
7. Cairns Craig, 'From the Lost Ground: Liz Lochhead, Douglas Dunn and Contemporary Scottish Poetry', in James Acheson and Romana Huk, ed., *Contemporary British Poetry: Essays in Theory and Criticism* (New York: SUNY Press, 1996), 343–372: 361.
8. See, respectively, Heaney, Seamus *Selected Poems 1965–1975* (London: Faber and Faber, 1980), 10; and Harrison, Tony *Selected Poems*, 2nd edition, (Harmondsworth: Penguin, 1987), 177–8.
9. See *Statutes of Liberty: The New York School of Poets* (Basingstoke: Palgrave, 2001), 122–4 for a useful discussion of the gender anxieties involved in men writing poetry.
10. In Acheson & Huk, 361.

CHAPTER THREE

1. Dunn, Douglas, 'Rhyme', *Poetry Wales*, 15.3, (Winter 1979–80), 39–41. Dunn's comments on 'a reversal of the standard myth of barbarism' also converge with Harrison's project in 'The Rhubar-

NOTES

barians' to 'raise / 'mob' *rhubarb-rhubarb* to a tribune's speech'. See Harrison, Tony, *Selected Poems* (Harmondsworth: Penguin, 1987), 113.
2. Wordsworth & Coleridge, *Lyrical Ballads*, R. L. Brett and A. R. Jones, eds., (London: Routledge, 1991), 241–272: 243. This edition uses the Preface of 1800 with 1802 variants added. Further references are given after quotations in the text.
3. Stevenson in *The Listener*, quoted in *RDD*, 73; Porter in *The Observer*, quoted on the inside front cover of the first paperback edition of *St. Kilda's Parliament*.
4. See Robert Hewison, *Too Much: Art and Society in the Sixties 1960–75* (London: Methuen, 1988), 294–7 for more details.
5. Reprinted as 'Towards a national debate', *Education*, 22 October 1976, 332–333. See 333 for the passage cited.
6. *British Poetry since 1970* (Manchester: Carcanet, 1980), xxvii.
7. Dunn, Douglas, 'The Grudge', *Stand*, 16.2, (1976), 4–6. Further references are given after quotations in the text.
8. It is important to recognize that this argument belongs to a particular historical moment. For mainstream writers of Dunn's generation there was only official culture in which to work, hence Dunn's 'grudge' and Harrison's similar bitterness over apparent exclusion. For British poets starting to write and publish after about 1980 there was a vital difference: the rise of the small press scene and the respectability of self-publication.
9. Easthope, Antony, *Poetry As Discourse* (London: Methuen, 1983), 68.
10. The idea that one man's culture is another man's labour is explored in 'Gardeners', 17–18.
11. Smout, T. C., *A Century of the Scottish People 1830–1950* (London: Collins, 1986), 238.
12. 'Adventure's Oafs', *Northlight*, (London: Faber and Faber, 1988), 80-1.
13. ' "As a man sees..." – on Norman MacCaig's poetry', *Verse* 7.2 (1990), 55–67: 59.
14. MacLaren, A. Allan, ed., *Social Class in Scotland: Past and Present* (Edinburgh: John Donald, 1976), 2 and 9 respectively.
15. See, respectively, *Northlight*, 28; and *Dante's Drum-kit*, 90.

CHAPTER FOUR

1. Corcoran, Neil, *English Poetry since 1940* (Harlow: Longman, 1993), 157.
2. The autobiographical trend is visible beyond elegiac poetry. Angela Huth's anthology *Well-Remembered Friends: Eulogies on*

Celebrated Lives (London: John Murray, 2004) collects euolgies from 1940 onwards. The earliest ones focus on a collective 'we' remembering public achievements while eulogies from the late 1990s onwards are much more personal and start with an individual speaker remembering the deceased's impact on his or her life.
3. University of Chicago Press, 2001, 159, original emphasis.
4. It is tempting to read this purely in terms of a sometimes anxious dialogue with male and female gender roles that surfaces intermittently in Dunn's poetry. However, in the context of returning delight, there may also be an echo of Wordsworth's female personification of creative and imaginative impulses in *The Prelude*. See Book I, lines 255–263; and Book II, lines 334–341.
5. See Chapter 2, note 5.
6. *The Kingfisher* (New York, Knopf, 1983), 29.
7. See *Collected Poems* (London: Macmillan, 1968). Page numbers in the following discussion refer to this edition.
8. Jahan Ramazani, *Poetry of Mourning: The Modern Elegy from Hardy to Heaney* (Chicago: University of Chicago Press, 1994), 68.
9. *Beyond Consolation: Death, Sexuality and the Changing Shapes of Elegy* (Ithaca: Cornell UP, 1997), 19. Further references are given after quotations in the text.
10. Harrison, Tony, *v.* (Newcastle upon Tyne: Bloodaxe Books, 1984); Reading, Peter, *Collected Poems 1: Poems 1970–1984* (Newcastle upon Tyne, Bloodaxe Books, 1995), 277–317; and Williams, Hugo, *Writing Home* (Oxford: OUP, 1985).
11. *The Deregulated Muse* (Newcastle upon Tyne: Bloodaxe Books, 1998), 28.
12. Craig, Cairns, 'From the Lost Ground: Liz Lochhead, Douglas Dunn and Contemporary Scottish Poetry', in Acheson, James and Romana Huk, eds, *Contemporary British Poetry: Essays in Theory and Criticism* (Albany: State University of New York Press, 1996), 343–372: 368.

CHAPTER FIVE

1. Bayley, John, 'A Poet more than Himself', *Poetry Review*, vol 84, no 2 (Summer 1994), 54–55: 55.
2. Heaney, Seamus *Wintering Out* (London: Faber and Faber, 1972), 31–3: 32.
3. 'On a hiding to nothing', *TLS*, January 26 2001: 23.

Select Bibliography

WORKS BY DOUGLAS DUNN

Terry Street (London: Faber & Faber, 1969).
The Happier Life (London: Faber & Faber, 1972).
Love or Nothing (London: Faber & Faber, 1974).
Two Decades of Irish Writing: A Critical Survey, as editor, (Cheadle Hulme: Carcanet, 1975).
Barbarians (London: Faber & Faber, 1979).
The Poetry of Scotland, as editor, (London: Batsford, 1979).
St. Kilda's Parliament (London: Faber & Faber, 1981).
A Rumoured City: New Poets from Hull, as editor, with a foreword by Philip Larkin (Newcastle upon Tyne: Bloodaxe Books, 1982).
To Build A Bridge: A celebration in verse of Humberside and its Bridge, as editor, (Lincoln: Lincoln & Humberside Arts, 1982).
Europa's Lover (Newcastle upon Tyne: Bloodaxe Books, 1982).
Elegies (London: Faber & Faber, 1985).
Secret Villages (London: Faber & Faber, 1985).
Selected Poems 1964–1983 (London: Faber & Faber, 1986).
Northlight, (London: Faber & Faber, 1988).
Racine's *Andromache*, as translator, (London: Faber & Faber, 1990).
Poll Tax: The Fiscal Fake (London: Chatto & Windus, 1990).
Scotland: An Anthology, as editor, (London: HarperCollins, 1991).
The Faber Book of Twentieth-Century Scottish Poetry, as editor, (London: Faber & Faber, 1992).
Dante's Drum-kit (London: Faber & Faber, 1993).
The Oxford Book of Scottish Short Stories, as editor, (Oxford: OUP, 1995).
Boyfriends and Girlfriends (London: Faber & Faber, 1996).
The Year's Afternoon (London: Faber & Faber, 2000).
The Donkey's Ears (London: Faber & Faber, 2000).
20th Century Scottish Poems, as editor, (London: Faber & Faber, 2000)
New Selected Poems 1964–1999 (London: Faber & Faber, 2003).

ARTICLES, CRITICISM AND REVIEWS

Douglas Dunn has published an enormous number of articles, editorials, criticism and reviews over the years. The following is a small selection of some of the more interesting and important pieces. A volume of *Collected Essays* is currently in preparation for Faber and Faber.

' "Finished fragrance": the poems of George Mackay Brown', *Poetry Nation* 2 (1974), 80–92.
'The Grudge', *Stand*, 16.2, (1976), 4–6.
'Make It Old', *Encounter*, 46, (May 1976), 75–81.
'Living Out of London – VIII', *London Magazine* 19 (5/6), August/September 1979, 71–9. Reminiscences of living in Hull.
' "Let the god not abandon us": on the poetry of Derek Mahon', *Stone Ferry Review* no. 2 (Winter 1978), 7–30.
'Three new poets: Douglas Dunn, Tom Paulin, Paul Mills' in P. R. King, editor, *Nine Contemporary Poets: A Critical Introduction*. Includes Dunn's own account of his poetic development, 221–8.
'Rhyme', *Poetry Wales*, 15.3, (Winter 1979–80), 39–41.
'The poetry of Alan Bold: Hammering on the Lyre', *Akros*, no. 42 (December 1979), 58–76.
'Hugh MacDiarmid: inhuman splendours', *New Edinburgh Review* no. 52 (November 1980), 17–21.
' "As a man sees" – on Norman MacCaig's poetry', *Verse* 7.2 (1990), 55–67.
'Morgan's sonnets.' In *About Edwin Morgan*, ed. Robert Crawford and Hamish Whyte (Edinburgh: EUP, 1990), 75–89.
'The Topical Muse', Kenneth Allott Lecture 1990 (Liverpool: Liverpool Classical Monthly 1990). Partially reprinted as 'Formal Strategies in Tony Harrison's Poetry', *Bloodaxe Critical Anthologies 1: Tony Harrison*, ed. by Neil Astley (Newcastle upon Tyne: Bloodaxe Books, 1991), 129–132.
'Importantly Live: Lyricism in Contemporary Poetry', inaugural lecture as Honorary Professor at Dundee University, 1987. (Dundee: Dundee University Occasional Papers No.1). Partially reprinted as 'Importantly Live: Harrison's Lyricism', in *Bloodaxe Critical Anthologies 1: Tony Harrison*, ed. by Neil Astley (Newcastle upon Tyne: Bloodaxe Books, 1991), 254–7.
'Abrasive encounters', in *Bloodaxe Critical Anthologies 1: Tony Harrison*, ed. by Neil Astley (Newcastle upon Tyne: Bloodaxe Books, 1991), 346–7.

INTERVIEWS

'A Different Drummer: Attila Dösa Interviews Douglas Dunn', *Poetry Review*, Vol 89 No 3, Autumn 1999: 27–34.
'Douglas Dunn talking with Robert Crawford', *Verse*, 4, (1985), 26–35.
Haffenden, John, Ed., *Viewpoints: Poets in Conversation* (London: Faber 7 Faber, 1981), 11–34.
'Interview with The Devil: Douglas Dunn', *The Printer's Devil*, A, (1990), 12–34.
Lee, J., 'Expansive lyricism', *Prelude: The Universities Arts Magazine* (Summer 1987), 14–19.
O'Donoghue, Bernard, 'An Interview with Douglas Dunn', *Oxford Poetry*, 2 2, (Spring 1985), 44–51.
Oxley, William, 'Interview with Douglas Dunn', *Acumen*, 13, (April 1991), 9–21.

CRITICAL STUDIES OF DOUGLAS DUNN

Ash, John, 'Pleasures of Invention, Rigours of Responsibility: Some notes on the poetry of Douglas Dunn', *PN Review*, Vol. 10, No. 2, 1983: 43–6.
Charlton, F. G., *Inalienable Perspectives: Douglas Dunn's Poetry 1963–83*. Newcastle upon Tyne: Newcastle University, 1984). 103 [Unpublished MA thesis]
Corcoran, Neil, 'Barbarians and Rhubarbarians: Douglas Dunn and Tony Harrison'. In his *English Poetry since 1940* (Harlow: Longman, 1993), 153–163.
Craig, Cairns, 'From the Lost Ground: Liz Lochhead, Douglas Dunn and Contemporary Scottish Poetry', in Acheson, James and Romana Huk, eds., *Contemporary British Poetry: Essays in Theory and Criticism* (Albany: State University of New York Press, 1996), 343–372.
Crawford, Robert, and David Kinloch, eds, *Reading Douglas Dunn* (Edinburgh: Edinburgh University Press, 1992). Contains interesting and insightful pieces by Ian Gregson, Sean O'Brien and Bernard O'Donoghue inter alia. The comprehensive bibliography (1963–1991) and the index should, however, be used with caution.
Fazzini, Marco, *Crossings: Essays on Contemporary Scottish Poetry and Hybridity*. (Venezia: Supernova, 2000). Contains an essay on Dunn and a bibliography.
Jarniewicz, Jerzy, *The Uses of the Commonplace in Contemporary British Poetry: Dunn, Larkin and Raine* (Łódź: University of Łódź Press, 1994). Includes a useful discussion of the similarities and differences

between Dunn and Larkin.

Kennedy, David, 'Voice and Ownership: Ideas of Individual Voice and Dominant Culture from 'Middle Generation' to 'New Generation'.' In his *New Relations: The Refashioning of British Poetry 1980–1994* (Bridgend: Seren, 1996), 24–54.

Kennedy, David, '"What does the fairy DO?" The staging of antithetical masculine styles in the poetry of Tony Harrison and Douglas Dunn', *Textual Practice* 14.1. (2000), 115–136.

Kennedy, David, 'Aesthetic Pain: Authenticity and Literary Anxiety in Douglas Dunn's *Elegies*' *English*, vol. 55, no. 213, Autumn 2006, 299–309.

Lyon, J. M., 'The art of grief: Douglas Dunn's *Elegies*.' *English*, vol. 40, no. 166, Spring 1991, 47–67.

O'Brien, Sean, 'Douglas Dunn: Ideology and Pastoral', in O'Brien, Sean, L. *The Deregulated Muse* (Newcastle upon Tyne: Bloodaxe Books, 1998), 65–80.

Osborne, John, et al, *Bête Noire, Terry Street* Special Edition, 16, (Autumn 1994).

Peach, Linden, 'A Politics of Being: The Poetry of Douglas Dunn.' In his *Ancestral Lines: Culture & Identity in the work of Six Contemporary Poets* (Bridgend: Seren, 1996), 134–153.

Robinson, Alan, 'The Mastering Eye: Douglas Dunn's Social Perceptions'. In his *Instabilities in Contemporary British Poetry* (Basingstoke: Macmillan, 1988), 82–99.

Smalley, Rebecca, *The Role of Memory in the poetry of Douglas Dunn and Tony Harrison with specific reference to elegy*. (Durham: University of Durham, 1991). [Unpublished Ph.D thesis]

Williams, D., '"They will not leave me, the lives of other people": the poetry of Douglas Dunn.' *Studies in Scottish Literature* 23, (1989), 1–24.

Index

Andrews, Lyman, 28
Arnold, Matthew, 56–7
Ash, John, 7

Bayley, John, 75
Bradbury, Malcolm, 24
Brogan, John, 67
Brown, George Mackay, 44–5, 48
Buchan, John, 34

Callaghan, James, 40
Campbell, Ian, 4
Camus, Albert, 38–9
Carducci, Gisouè, 57
Clampitt, Amy, 59–60
Conquest, Robert, 3
Corcoran, Neil, 1–2, 20, 55–6
Cox, C. B., 40
Craig, Cairns, 1, 32, 68
Crawford, Robert, 46, 48, 49, 56, 63–4, 77

Derrida, Jacques, 58
Desnos, Robert, 55, 56
Dösa, Attila, 76, 80
Dryden, John, 27
Dunn, Douglas,
 'A Game of Bowls', 74
 'A Poem in Praise of the British', 20–21, 35, 71
 'A Removal from Terry Street', 2, 15–16
 'A Window Affair', 12, 17, 18
 'Abernethy', 63, 65

'Academy's Runners', 70
'Adventure's Oafs', 67–8
'Alice', 44
'After the War', 27–28
'An Address on the Destitution of Scotland', 48, 49
'An Artist Waiting in a Country House', 40, 42
Andromache, 70
'Anniversaries', 61
'Arrangements', 59
'At Cruggleton Castle', 61
'At Falkland Palace', 63, 64
'At a Yorkshire Bus–stop', 26, 27
'Audenesques for 1960', 53, 74
'Australian Dream–Essay', 71
'Backwaters', 25
'Bagni di Lucca', 71
'Ballad of the Two Left Hands', 43
Barbarians, 37–45, 64, 66, 75
'Barbarian Pastorals', 38, 39, 42
"Bare Ruined Choirs", 72
'Bedfordshire', 71
'Bete Noire's Edition of *Terry Street'*, 78, 79, 80
'Body Echoes', 73
'Boys with Coats', 33–4
'Broughty Ferry', 65
'Caledonian Moonlight', 35
'Chateau d'If', 61
'Close of Play', 1

INDEX

'Clydesiders', 31, 32–3
'Creatures', 60, 61
Dante's Drum–kit, 46, 51, 52, 70–6
'Daylight', 63, 65
'December', 62
'December's Door', 66–7
'Dining', 58–9
'Disenchantments', 71, 71–2
'Dressed to Kill', 70, 75–6
'Drowning', 44
'Early Autumn', 74
'East Riding', 79–80
Elegies, 36, 54, 56–63
'Elegy for the Lost Parish', 44
'Empires', 43
'Empty Wardrobes', 61
Europa's Lover, 55
Faber Book of Twentieth–Century Scottish Poetry, The, 45–6, 70
'Five Years Married', 26
'Fixed', 27, 49
'Gaberlunzie', 72
'Galloway Motor Farm', 49
'Gardeners', 42
'Glasgow Schoolboys, Running Backwards', 6, 44
'Going to Aberlemno', 63, 65
'Going to Bed', 35
'Green Breeks', 34, 45, 50, 52–3
'Guerillas', 27–8
'Here and There', 14, 45, 53, 65–6, 67
'Here Be Dragons', 37, 40, 42
'Hush', 60
'Indolence', 78
'In the 1950s', 67, 69
'In The Grounds', 37, 40
'Jig of the Week No.21', 67
'John Wilson in Greenock, 1786', 45, 50, 51
'Just Standing There', 75
'Kabla Khun', 70–1
'Lamp–posts', 54
'Landscape with One Figure', 20
'Leaving Dundee', 63
'Leisure No End', 26
'Leopardi', 79
'Libraries: A Celebration', 71
'Little Rich Rhapsody', 29
Love or Nothing, 28–36, 43, 65, 69
'Love–making by Candlelight', 64, 66, 68
'Maggie's Corner', 67, 69
'Memory and Imagination', 67–8
'Men of Terry Street', 1, 2, 10
'Middle Age', 74
'Midweek Matinee', 25
'Modern Love', 23
'Moorlander', 72
'New Light on Terry Street', 13
'Nineteen–Thirteen', 72
Northlight, 45, 52, 63–69, 71
'On Roofs of Terry Street', 26
'One Thing and Another', 74
'On Whether Loneliness Ever Has a Beginning', 79–80
'Out of Breath', 80
Poll Tax: The Fiscal Fake, 69, 73
'Poor People's Cafés', 69, 73
'Portrait Photograph, 1915', 44
'Preserve and Renovate', 71, 75
'Pushkin's Ring', 79
'Queen February', 72
'Reading Pascal in the Lowlands', 59–60
'Realisms', 31, 34
'Renfrewshire Traveller', 6, 31, 34, 35
'Re–reading Katherine Mansfield's *Bliss and Other Stories*', 58
'Rose', 54

INDEX

'Restraint', 34–5
'Running the East Wind', 67
'S. Frediano's', 63, 64
St Kilda's Parliament, 7, 34, 45–54, 63, 64, 65, 73
'St Kilda's Parliament: 1879–1979', 46–8
'Saturday Night Function', 23
'Stranger's Grief', 66
'Sunday Morning Among The Houses of Terry Street', 19
'Swigs', 73–4
'Syndrome', 6, 27
'Tannahill', 45, 50–1
'Teachers', 98
Terry Street, 2, 9–21, 24, 35, 43, 46–7, 62, 68
'The Apple–Tree', 6, 48
'The Clear Day', 59
'The Clothes Pit', 2, 10–13, 29
'The Come–on', 6, 38–40, 42, 44
'The Competition', 33–4, 38, 40
'The Concert', 35
'The Crossroads of the Birds', 72–3
'The Dark Crossroads', 6, 67–8
'The Departures of Friends in Childhood', 69
'The Dilemma', 34
'The Disguise', 34–5
The Donkey's Ears, 76–8
'The Estuarial Republic', 34, 69
'The Friendship of Young Poets', 26
'The Garden', 24–5, 27, 29, 75
'The Grudge', 40–2
The Happier Life, 6, 22–28, 29, 43, 55, 75
'The Happier Life', 27
'The Harp of Renfrewshire', 49–50, 51, 54, 63, 65
'The House Next Door', 29
'The Hunched', 25
'The Local', 73
'The Malediction', 34
'The Miniature Metro', 53–4
'The Musical Orchard', 26, 55
'The Musician', 43–4
'The Opportunity', 34
'The Patricians', 10
'The Penny Gibbet', 72
'The People Before', 63, 64
'The River Through The City', 25
'The Silences', 1, 11, 17, 18
'The Stories', 58
'The Student', 37, 40, 42
'The Terry Street Fusiliers', 13–14
'The War in the Congo', 67
'The White Poet', 35
'Thirteen Steps and the Thirteenth of March', 59
'Three Poets', 79
'Turn Over a New Leaf', 70
'Tursac', 58
'Under The Stone', 25–6, 28
'Variations on the Words 'Solo' and 'Exhaust'', 35
'Washing the Coins', 49
'Watches of Grandfathers', 44
'Weeding a Border', 6, 74
'White Fields', 31, 33
'Winkie', 67
'Winter Graveyard', 29–30, 50, 65
'Winter Orchard', 29–31, 34, 36
'Witch–girl', 49–50, 53
'Woodnotes', 79
'Writing with Light', 58
The Year's Afternoon, 78–80
'The Year's Afternoon', 96
'Young Women in Rollers', 2, 12, 17–18, 25
Dyson, A. E., 40

INDEX

Easthope, Anthony, 40

Fuller, John, 9

Gray, Thomas, 57, 62, 66
Gregson, Ian, 2, 4, 16

Haffenden, John, 11, 18–19, 23, 24, 27, 31, 44, 50, 55, 65
Hamilton, Ian, 9, 24
Hamilton, Paul, 57
Hardy, Thomas, 60–1
    'A Circular', 60–1
    'A Death–Day Recalled', 61
    'A Dream or No', 61
    'At Castle Boterel', 61
    'The Haunter', 61
    'The Shadow on the Stone', 60
    'Your Last Drive', 61
Harrison, Tony, 6, 32, 41, 62
Heaney, Seamus, 4, 5, 6, 24, 32, 41, 53, 76
Heath, Edward, 24, 40
Henry IV Part II, 15
Henry V, 92
Hechter, Michael, 5–6
Herbert, W. N., 6, 46, 63, 70
Hill, Geoffrey, 24, 60
Hogg, James, 4
Horace, 1, 30
Hughes, Ted, 24

Jamie, Kathleen, 88
Jones, Peter, 40

Keats, John, 67
Kinloch, David, 39

Laforgue, Jules, 37, 55
Larkin, Philip, 3, 9, 20, 22, 26, 66, 67
Lindsay, Maurice, 22
Lodge, David, 24

Longley, Edna, 7
Lowell, Robert, 66
Luxembourg, Rosa, 3

MacCaig, Norman, 49
MacLaren, A. Allan, 52
MacLean, Sorley, 98
Mahon, Derek, 31
Mangan, Gerald, 96, 98
Marvell, Andrew, 27, 30
Milton, John, 57–8, 62
Morrison, Blake, 20
Muir, Edwin, 46, 67

New Lines, 3
Nizan, Paul, 38–9, 55

O'Brien, Sean, 3, 6–7, 10, 31, 34, 37, 53, 66, 68
O'Donoghue, Bernard, 5, 23, 29, 31, 33, 36, 54, 56, 62
Osborne, John, 13
Oxley, William, 3, 5, 26, 43, 56, 57

Pope, Alexander, 27
Porter, Peter, 28–9, 39–40

Raban, Jonathan, 9, 10
Racine, 64
Ramazani, Jahan, 60
Reading, Peter, 62
Robinson, Alan, 22
Rushdie, Salman, 4

Schmidt, Michael, 40
Scott, Sir Walter, 4, 46, 64
Shelley, Percy Bysshe, 57
Smith, Dave, 60
Smout, T. C., 44
Stabler, Jane, 5, 11
Stevenson, Anne, 39
Stevenson, Robert Louis, 4
Swinburne, Charles Algernon, 56

Tennyson, Alfred, 57, 60
Thatcher, Margaret, 40
Theocritus, 57
Twelfth Night, 15

Virgil, 30

Ward, Geoff, 32
Williams, Hugo, 9, 62
Williams, Raymond, 12
Wordsworth, William, 37–8, 41–2

Zeiger, Melissa F., 60–2

www.ingramcontent.com/pod-product-compliance
Lightning Source LLC
Chambersburg PA
CBHW030147240426
43672CB00005B/301